PHOTOSHOP 5.5

in easy steps

ROBERT SHUFFLEBOTHAM

In easy steps is an imprint of Computer Step
Southfield Road. Southam
Warwickshire CV47 OFB. England

Tel: 01926 817999 Fax: 01926 817005
http://www.computerstep.com

Notice of Liability

Every effort has been made to ensure that this book contains accurate
and current information. However, Computer Step and the author shall
not be liable for any loss or damage suffered by readers as a result of
any information contained herein.

Trademarks

Photoshop®, Illustrator®, InDesign®, PageMaker® and PostScript® are
registered trademarks of Adobe Systems Incorporated. All other
trademarks are acknowledged as belonging to their respective
companies.

Printed and bound in the United Kingdom

ISBN 1-84078-084-3

Contents

1 Basic Theory

Bitmaps and Vectors	8
Pixels and Resolution	10
RGB and CMYK Colour Models	11
RGB Setup	14
CMYK Setup	15
Greyscale Setup	17
Monitor Calibration	18

2 The Working Environment

The Photoshop Screen Environment	22
Using the Toolbox	24
Document and Scratch Sizes	26
Ruler Guides and Grids	27
Moving Around	28
The Info Palette	29
Palette Techniques	30
Saving and Loading Custom Settings	32
Printing Composites – Mac	33
Printing Composites – Windows	35
The History Palette	36
Deleting, Clearing & Purging States	37
Taking Snapshots	38

3 Opening and Saving Files

Opening Images in Photoshop	40
Scanning into Photoshop	41
Opening Photo CD Images	42
Opening an EPS File	44
Placing an EPS File	45
Saving Files	46
TIFF Format	47
Photoshop EPS	48
JPEG Format	49
Creating a New File	50

4 Getting Started with Images

Rotating an Image	52
Resizing without Resampling	53
Resampling Up	54
Sampling Down	56
Cropping an Image	58
Adding a Border	59
Image Modes	60
Duotone Mode	62

5 Defining Colours

Foreground and Background Colours	64
The Eyedropper and Colour Sampler Tools (I)	65
The Colour Picker Palette	66
Selecting Pantone Colours	68
The Colour Palette	69
The Swatches Palette	70

6 The Painting Tools

The Brushes Palette	72
Painting Tool Techniques and Settings	74
The Paintbrush Tool (B)	76
The Airbrush Tool (J)	77
The Pencil and Line Tools (N)	78
The Gradient Tool (G)	80
The Paint Bucket Tool (K)	81
Blending Modes	82
Defining a Brush	84

7 The Editing Tools

The Blur, Sharpen and Smudge Tools (R)	86
The Rubber and Pattern Stamp Tools (S)	88
The Dodge, Burn and Sponge Tools (O)	90
The Eraser Tool (E)	92
The Magic Eraser (E)	93
The Background Eraser (E)	95

8 Making Selections

The Marquee Selection Tool (M)	98
Marquee Options	99
Moving Selections	100
The Lasso Tools (L)	102
The Magic Wand Tool (W)	105
Feathering Selections	106
Modifying Selections	108
The Grow and Similar Commands	109
Pasting Into Selections	110
The Defringe Command	111
Filling a Selection	112
Copying and Pasting Selections	113
Transforming Selections	114

9 Layers

Working with Layers	116
Merging and Flattening Layers	118
Moving Layers Between Images	119
Linking Layers	120
Adjustment Layers	121

Transparency | 123
New Layer Commands | 124
Layer Effects | 125
Managing Layer Effects | 127
Transforming Layers | 129
The Extract Command | 131
Fine Tuning Extractions | 134

10 Working with Type

Creating Type | 136
Type Settings | 138
Editing and Selecting Type | 140
Vertical and Rotated Type | 142
Type Mask Tools | 143
Type and Layer Effects | 144

11 Paths

Converting Selections to Paths | 146
Creating Paths Using the Pen Tool | 148
Showing and Selecting Paths and Points | 150
Adding, Deleting and Converting Points | 151
Creating Corner Points | 152
Editing Points | 153
Exporting Clipping Paths | 154
Exporting Paths to Adobe Illustrator | 156

12 Channels and Masks

Quick Mask Mode | 158
The Channels Palette | 159
Saving and Loading Selections | 160
Editing Alpha Channel Masks | 162
Layer Masks | 164
Channel and Quick Mask Options | 166

13 Colour Correction Techniques

The Brightness/Contrast Command | 168
The Auto Levels Command | 169
The Levels Dialogue Box | 170
The Curves Dialogue Box | 172
The Colour Balance Dialogue Box | 174

14 Filters

Filter Controls | 176
Unsharp Mask and Sharpen Filters | 177
Blur Filters | 179
Noise Filters | 181
Filter Samples | 183

15 Web and Multimedia Images

Save for Web – 2Up	186
Optimisation: 4-Up View	188
Preview and Save Optimised Images	190
Indexed Colour Mode	192
Colour Palettes	193
Dithering	195
Saving Indexed Colour Images as GIFs	196
Exporting RGB Images in GIF Format	197
JPEG Format for Web Images	199
PNG File Format	200

16 Working with Image Ready

Photoshop and ImageReady	202
The ImageReady Toolbox & Image Window	203
Jumping Between Applications	204
Creating and Saving Images	206
Layer Effects in ImageReady	208
Handling Type in ImageReady	210
Rectangle and Ellipse Tools	212
The ImageReady Optimise Palette	213
Saving an Optimised Image	215

17 Animations

Creating a Simple Animation	218
Playing and Managing Frames	220
Optimising and Saving Animations	222
Tweening	224
Copying and Pasting Frames	226

18 Slicing Images

Slices from Guides and the Slice Tool	228
Creating Slices from Selections	230
User- and Auto-slices	231
Working with Slices	232
Assigning URLs to Slices	234

Index	235

Basic Theory

An understanding of the basics of colour is important if you are to get the best out of Photoshop. Refer back to this section from time to time. As your understanding of Photoshop grows, so will your appreciation of the concepts of colour that underpin the whole process of image capture and image manipulation.

This section also covers RGB, CMYK and Greyscale setup options and monitor calibration.

Covers

Bitmaps and Vectors | 8

Pixels and Resolution | 10

RGB and CMYK Colour Models | 11

RGB Setup | 14

CMYK Setup | 15

Greyscale Setup | 17

Monitor Calibration | 18

Chapter One

Bitmaps and Vectors

Photoshop is an image-editing application with a wealth of tools and commands for working on digital images or bitmaps. There are utilities for retouching, colour correcting, compositing and more. There are also over 90 functional and creative filters that can be applied to entire images, or selected areas within images.

A bitmap image consists of a rectangular grid, or raster, of pixels – in concept, very much like a mosaic. When you edit a bitmap you are editing the colour values of individual pixels or groups of pixels.

Image-editing applications differ fundamentally from vector-based applications such as Adobe Illustrator and Macromedia FreeHand. In these applications, you work with objects that can be moved, scaled, transformed, stacked and deleted as individual or grouped objects, but all the time each exists as a complete, separate object.

These applications are called vector drawing packages, as each object is defined by a mathematical formula. Because of this, they are resolution-independent – you can scale vector drawings up or down (either in the originating application or in a page layout application such as QuarkXPress or Adobe PageMaker) and they will still print smoothly and crisply.

You should always try to scan an image at, or slightly larger than, the size at which you intend to use it. This means you will avoid having to increase the size of the image.

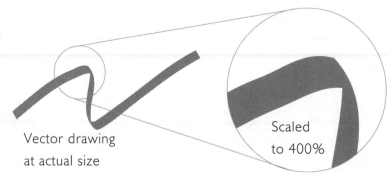

Vector drawing
at actual size

Scaled
to 400%

In contrast, bitmaps are created at a set resolution – a fixed number of pixels per inch. If you scan an image at a specific resolution, then double its size, you are effectively halving its resolution (unless you add more pixels). You are likely to end up with a blocky, jagged image, as you have increased the size of the individual pixels that make up the bitmap image.

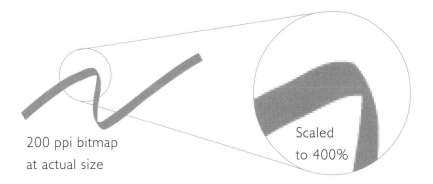

200 ppi bitmap
at actual size

Scaled
to 400%

Bitmaps and Bit-depth

An important factor when the digital data for an image is captured, typically at the scanning stage, is its bit-depth. Bit-depth refers to the amount of digital storage space used to record information about the colour of a pixel. The more bits you use, the more colour information you can store to describe the colour of a pixel – but also, the larger the file size you end up with.

More, rather than less, colour information is usually desirable, as this means the image can represent more shades of colour, with finer transitions between colours and greater density of colour, leading to a more realistic image.

To output realistic images using PostScript technology an image should be able to represent 256 grey levels. A 24-bit scan is sufficient for recording 256 grey levels for each of the Red, Green and Blue channels, resulting in a possible combination of over 16 million colours.

Ideally, when you work on images in Photoshop you will do so using a 24-bit monitor capable of displaying over 16 million colours. This ensures that you see all the colour detail in the image. Although you can work on images using only thousands of colours, for best results, especially where colour reproduction is important, you need to work with as many colours as possible.

Pixels and Resolution

Pixels

A pixel is the smallest element in a bitmap image such as a scan. Pixel is short for 'picture element'. Zoom in on an image in Photoshop and you will start to see the individual pixels – the fundamental building blocks – that make up the image. When working in Photoshop, you are editing pixels, changing their colour, shade and brightness.

Resolution

A key factor when working on bitmap images is resolution. This is measured in pixels per inch (ppi).

Pixels can vary in size. If you have an image with a resolution of 100 ppi, each pixel would be 1/100th of an inch square. In an image with a resolution of 300 ppi, each pixel would be 1/300th of an inch square – giving a much finer, less blocky result.

Printer resolution measured in dots per inch (dpi) is not the same as image resolution measured in pixels per inch (ppi). Printer dots are a fixed size, pixels can vary in size.

When working on images that will eventually be printed on a printing press, you need to work on high-resolution images. These are scanned images whose resolution is twice the halftone screen frequency (measured in lines per inch – lpi) that will be used for final output – that is when you output to bromide or film.

For example, for a final output screen frequency of 150 lpi – a typical screen frequency used for glossy magazines – you need to scan your image at a resolution of 300 ppi.

Resolutions of double the screen frequency are important for images with fine lines, repeating patterns or textures. You can achieve acceptable results, especially when printing at screen frequencies greater than 133 lpi, using resolutions of 1½ times the final screen frequency.

Images intended for multimedia presentations or the World Wide Web need only be 72 ppi, which is effectively the screen resolution.

To work with images for positional purposes only, as long as you can get accurate enough on-screen results and laser proofs, you can work with much lower resolutions.

RGB and CMYK Colour Models

As you start working with Adobe Photoshop there are two colour models that you need to be aware of. These are the RGB (Red, Green, Blue) and CMYK (Cyan, Magenta, Yellow and BlacK) colour models.

RGB is important because it mirrors the way the human eye perceives colour. It is the model used by scanners and digital cameras to capture colour information in digital format, and it is the way that your computer monitor describes colour.

Red, green and blue are referred to as the **additive primaries**. You can add varying proportions of the three colours to produce millions of different colours – but still a more limited range (or 'gamut') than in nature, due to the limitations of the phosphor screen coating of the monitor. If you add 100% red, green and blue light together, you get white. You produce the **secondary** colours when you add red and blue to get magenta; green and blue to get cyan; red and green to get yellow.

The CMYK colour model is referred to as the **subtractive** colour model. It is important because this is the colour model used by printing presses.

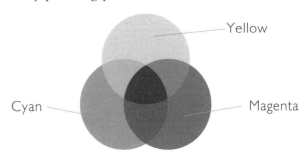

If you subtract all cyan, magenta and yellow when printing you end up with the complete absence of colour – white.

On the printing press, cyan, magenta, yellow and black are combined to simulate a huge variety of colours. Printers add black because, although in theory, if you combine 100% each of cyan, magenta and yellow you produce black, in reality, because of impurities in the dyes, you only get a muddy brown.

Colour Gamuts

Colour gamut refers to the range of colours that a specific device is capable of producing. There are millions of colours in the visible spectrum that the eye can discern. Scanners, monitors and printing presses cannot reproduce every colour in the visible spectrum – the range of colours they are capable of producing is their gamut.

From the desktop publishing point of view, the process of capturing digital colour information, viewing and manipulating this on-screen and then finally printing the image using coloured inks is complicated, because the gamut of a colour monitor is different to the gamut of CMYK and Pantone inks.

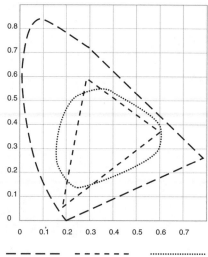

Visible Spectrum   Monitor   SWOP-CMYK

There are colours (especially vibrant yellows and deep blues) that can be displayed on a monitor but cannot be printed using traditional CMYK inks.

Typically, when you work in Photoshop, you will work in RGB (Red, Green, Blue) mode. RGB mode is faster to work in than CMYK mode, and in RGB mode all Photoshop options and commands are available to you. When you have finished making necessary adjustments and corrections to the image, you will need to convert it to CMYK mode, before saving/exporting the image in EPS or TIFF format for use in a page layout application such as Adobe PageMaker or QuarkXPress.

When you convert from RGB to CMYK mode, Photoshop converts out-of-gamut colours (in this case, colours that can be seen on screen, but not printed) into their nearest printable equivalent.

RGB Setup

RGB setup allows you to define a device-independent colour space in which to work. In previous versions of Adobe Photoshop, the RGB working space was that of the monitor. When images were viewed on different monitors the results could prove unpredictable.

When you choose an option from the RGB pop-up, the Gamma, White Point and Primaries change automatically. Don't change these settings unless you have considerable knowledge and experience of colour printing.

To set the RGB workspace, choose File > Colour Settings > RGB Setup. Choose an RGB workspace for your image from the RGB pop-up.
Sticking with the default colour space (sRGB) is a safe bet if you are new to colour management and it is not your main concern at the outset, or if you

are working with images intended for the Web or multimedia. Choose Apple RGB if you want to use the same RGB colour space that previous versions of Adobe Photoshop used as a default. ColorMatch RGB (based on the Radius PressView display) is commonly regarded as a good choice for professional publishers as it comes closest to matching the range of colours that can typically be reproduced in print and displayed on monitors.

It is important that anyone else viewing the same image does so on a correctly calibrated monitor and using the same RGB workspace if colours are to be viewed accurately and consistently on different monitors.

2 Select the Display Using Monitor Compensation option so that when you open an image it is converted to your monitor's RGB colour space for the current work session.

CMYK Setup

CMYK Setup options are important to ensure correct and predictable results when you convert RGB images to CMYK for print. Use the Built-in option if you are an experienced Photoshop user and familiar with the options available, or if you have been told by your commercial printer the appropriate settings to use. If you are new to Photoshop and colour management, the ICC option is probably the best choice.

An ICC (International Colour Consortium) profile defines the colour space for a specific device (eg, a printer or a monitor).

Profiles are stored in System\Preferences\ColorSync Profiles (Mac), Windows\System\Colour folder (Windows). You may have to obtain the correct profiles before you can select them. Try www.apple.com/colorsync or www.microsoft.com/hwtest/hcl/ as starting points for locating appropriate printer profiles. Alternatively, try the web site of the printer manufacturer.

1 To set CMYK options choose File > Colour Settings > CMYK Setup. Click the ICC options at the top of the CMYK Setup dialogue box.

2 Use the Profile pop-up to choose the profile of the actual printer you will be using.

If you are using an RGB printer (eg, a low end inkjet printer) there is no need to enter CMYK setup information.

Adobe has a useful section at its Website which deals in more detail with Photoshop's colour management options: www.adobe.com/ supportservice/custsupport/ TECHGUIDE/PSHOP/ main.html

3 Choose a Colour Management Module (CMM) from the Engine pop-up. The CMM is the software colour management module that brings the various ICC colour profiles together and manages colour to ensure device independent colour management. Built-in refers to the Adobe Photoshop built-in CMM and is a good choice for beginners.

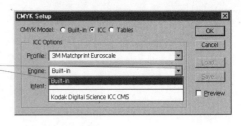

4 Leave the Intent pop-up on Perceptual. This option preserves the original relationships from colour to colour and achieves the most natural result.

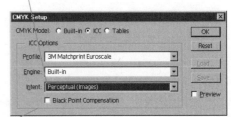

5 Leave the Black Point Compensation option unchecked.

6 Click the Preview option to see the results of your selections in any open image windows.

Greyscale Setup

If you are working with greyscale images you need to decide how the image will be treated.

1 To set Greyscale options, choose File > Colour Settings > Greyscale Setup.

Dot Gain refers to the expected increase in size of a halftone dot (between film and final output) caused by the spread of ink as it is absorbed by paper.

2 Select the RGB option if your images are intended for the World Wide Web or multimedia use. The RGB option creates a composite grey which consists of equal amounts of red, green and blue light. There is no compensation for dot gain when you use this setting.

3 Choose Black Ink if your images will be printed. The Black Ink setting is based on the settings in the CMYK Setup dialogue box. The greys in the image behave like the black plate in a CMYK image. This option includes compensation for dot gain.

4 Select the Preview option if you have an image open and you want to see how the different settings affect the image.

Monitor Calibration

It is important to calibrate your monitor so that colours in your image are displayed accurately. Calibrating your monitor should eliminate any colour casts (typically reddish or blueish) on your monitor and ensure that the monitor displays greys as neutrally as possible.

Use the Adobe Gamma utility to calibrate the monitor you are using and to define the RGB colour space that your monitor can display.

Once you have calibrated your monitor, Photoshop can compensate for the differences between the colour space in which your image resides and the colour space of the monitor you are using.

The Adobe Gamma utility enables you to calibrate the contrast and brightness, gamma (midtones), colour balance and the white point of the monitor. Calibration settings that you create are saved as an ICC (International Colour Consortium) profile with a .icm extension.

Use the Adobe Gamma Wizard if you are do not have previous experience of calibrating a monitor.

For monitor calibration to be effective, you should not adjust the brightness and contrast settings on your monitor after you have completed the calibration process, and you must ensure that the lighting conditions within the room remain constant.

1 (Windows) Choose Settings > Control Panel from the Start Menu. Double-click the Adobe Gamma icon to display the dialog.
(Macintosh) Use the Apple menu to choose Control Panel > Adobe Gamma.

2 Choose Step by Step Wizard, then click the Next button.

Leave your monitor turned on for at least 30 minutes before you calibrate. This allows the phosphors time to warm up fully and for the display to stabilise.

3 Click the Load button to choose a monitor profile which matches the monitor you are using most closely. (Windows) Profiles are stored in the Windows\ System\ Colour folder. (Mac) Profiles are stored in the System\Preferences\ColorSync Profiles folder. Profiles should be available from your monitor manufacturer's Web site, or you can try: www.microsoft.com/hwtest/hcl/. Click the Next button.

4 Adjust the Brightness and Contrast settings of your monitor. Refer to the monitor handbook if you are unsure of how to adjust these settings. Click the Next button.

5 Only change the Phosphors pop-up if you know that your monitor's phosphors are different from the default selection. Click the Next button.

6   With the View Single Gamma Only option selected, drag the Gamma slider until the square in the middle of the patterned lines fades, as far as possible, into the pattern. This defines the brightness of the midtones on your monitor. (Un-focus your eyes slightly to help achieve the correct result.) Click the Next button.

7   For Desired Gamma choose a target gamma. This option is not available on Windows systems which cannot control the monitor. If you intend to prepare images for the World Wide Web or multimedia presentations, choose a gamma of 2.2. If you intend to print images using CMYK inks, you typically choose a gamma of 1.8. Click the Next button.

8   Leave the Hardware White Point on the default setting unless you know this to be inaccurate. Click the Next button.

9   Leave Adjusted White Point on Same as Hardware unless you want to view the image at a different colour temperature to that set by the monitor's factory specified setting. Click the Next button.

10   Click the Finish button to save settings as an .icm compatible profile.

The Working Environment

This section covers the basics of the Photoshop working environment, getting you used to the Photoshop window, the Toolbox, palettes and a number of standard Photoshop conventions that you will find useful as you develop your Photoshop skills.

It also covers the basics of printing composite images to a PostScript laser printer as well as techniques for undoing commands as you work on your images.

Covers

The Photoshop Screen Environment | 22

Using the Toolbox | 24

Document and Scratch Sizes | 26

Ruler Guides and Grids | 27

Moving Around | 28

The Info Palette | 29

Palette Techniques | 30

Saving and Loading Custom Settings | 32

Printing Composites – Mac | 33

Printing Composites – Windows | 35

The History Palette | 36

Deleting, Clearing & Purging States | 37

Taking Snapshots | 38

Chapter Two

The Photoshop Screen Environment

There are three 'screen modes' to choose from when working on images in Photoshop. The screen mode icons are located at the bottom of the toolbox. Full screen with menu bar mode is useful when working on individual images because it clears away the clutter of the Finder environment (Mac) or the Windows desktop. Use Full screen mode to see the image without the distraction of other screen elements, and without any other colours interfering with the colours in your image.

Standard screen mode

Full screen
with menu bar
mode

Full screen mode

1 Click this icon to return to Standard screen mode.

2 Click this icon to go to Full screen with menu bar mode.

3 Click this icon to go to Full screen mode. Press the Tab key to hide/show the toolbox and palettes.

4 Click the Jump To button to launch ImageReady. (See page 204).

Command (often referred to as 'Apple' on the Mac) and Ctrl (Windows), and alt (Mac) and Alt (Windows) are used identically as modifier keys. Shift is standard on both platforms.

Windows Environment

The Windows environment offers identical functionality to the Macintosh environment, as you can see from a comparison of the Windows and Macintosh screen shots.

Windows users can use the right mouse button to access context sensitive menus; Mac users can hold down the ctrl key and press their single mouse button.

The Image Window

You need the rulers showing to create ruler guides. Use the shortcut Command/Ctrl + R to show or hide rulers.

Title bar

Close box

Image

Rulers

Scroll bars

Sizes bar

View Percentage

Resize box

Using the Toolbox

There are a number of useful general techniques that relate to choosing tools in the Toolbox, including those from the expanded range of hidden tool pop-ups.

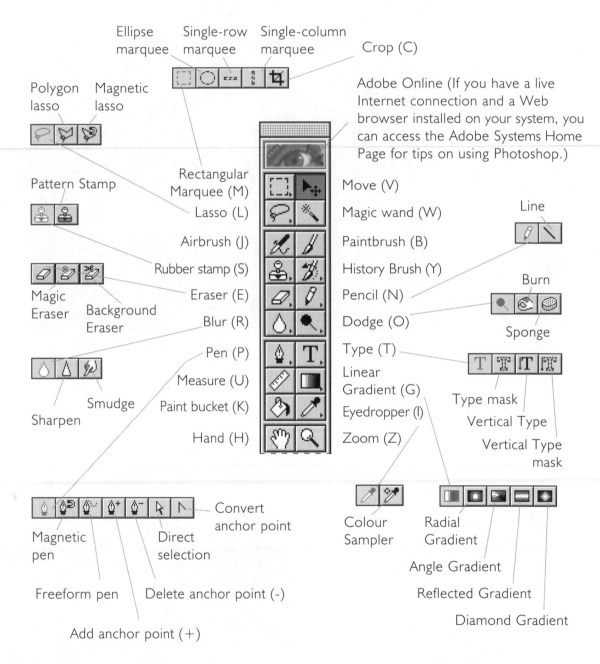

Ellipse marquee
Single-row marquee
Single-column marquee
Crop (C)

Polygon lasso
Magnetic lasso

Adobe Online (If you have a live Internet connection and a Web browser installed on your system, you can access the Adobe Systems Home Page for tips on using Photoshop.)

Pattern Stamp

Rectangular Marquee (M)
Lasso (L)
Airbrush (J)
Rubber stamp (S)
Eraser (E)
Blur (R)
Pen (P)
Measure (U)
Paint bucket (K)
Hand (H)

Move (V)
Magic wand (W)
Paintbrush (B)
History Brush (Y)
Pencil (N)
Dodge (O)
Type (T)
Linear Gradient (G)
Eyedropper (I)
Zoom (Z)

Line

Burn

Sponge

Magic Eraser
Background Eraser

Sharpen
Smudge

Type mask
Vertical Type
Vertical Type mask

Magnetic pen
Direct selection
Convert anchor point

Freeform pen
Delete anchor point (-)

Add anchor point (+)

Colour Sampler
Radial Gradient

Angle Gradient

Reflected Gradient

Diamond Gradient

...cont'd

Foreground colour — Switch colours (X)

Default colours (D) — Background colour

Standard mode (Q) — Quick Mask mode (Q)

Standard screen mode (F) — Full screen mode (F)

Full screen mode with menu bar (F)

Jump To button

Double-click on a tool to show the appropriate Options palette for that tool.

1 Press the keyboard shortcut (in brackets) to access tools.

2 Click and hold on any tool with a small triangle in the bottom right corner to see all tools in that tool group.

3 Hold down alt/Alt and click on any tool in a tool group to cycle through the available tools. Alternatively, hold down Shift, then press the keyboard shortcut for that tool group a number of times. For example, press 'O' three times to cycle through all the tools in the Dodge tool group.

Use Display & Cursor Preferences in the File menu to change the default appearance of painting and other Cursors.

4 Press Tab to hide/show all palettes, including the toolbox. Hold down Shift, then press the Tab key to hide/show all palettes except the Toolbox.

5 Press Caps Lock to change painting cursors to a precise crosshair cursor, which indicates the centre of the painting tool. Press Caps Lock again to return to standard cursors.

Document and Scratch Sizes

The Sizes Bar is useful for monitoring disk space and memory considerations as you work on your images.

Document Sizes

With Document Sizes selected, you will see two numbers separated by a slash. The first number is the size of the image when all layers are flattened. The second number may be larger and represents the file storage size, whilst the image contains additional layers

and/or alpha channels you may have set up. In images that consist of only a single layer, with no additional channels, both numbers are the same.

Scratch Sizes

Use the Plug-ins & Scratch Disk preferences (File > Preferences) to specify the hard disk you want Photoshop to use as a Scratch disk.

The Scratch disk is an underlying technical detail that you should be aware of when using Photoshop. The Scratch disk is a designated hard disk that Photoshop utilises as 'virtual' memory if it runs out of memory (RAM) whilst working on one or more images.

With Scratch Sizes selected in the Sizes Bar you again see two numbers separated by a slash. The first number represents the amount of memory (RAM) Photoshop needs to handle all currently open pictures. The second number represents the actual amount of memory available to Photoshop. When the first number is greater than the second, Photoshop is using the Scratch disk as virtual memory.

(Macintosh) Switch off Virtual Memory in the Memory control panel. Photoshop uses its own virtual memory management system to work with the Scratch disk.

As a general rule of thumb when working in Photoshop, you should have free disk space of at least 3–5 times the file size of the image you are working on. This is because Photoshop makes use of the Scratch disk as virtual memory and because Photoshop needs to hold more than one copy of the image you are working on for the Undo, Revert and From Saved commands.

Ruler Guides and Grids

You can show a grid in your image window to help with alignment and measuring, and you can also drag in ruler guides from the rulers. Both sets of guides are non-printing.

You can customise the appearance of the grid and guides using File > Preferences > Guides & Grid.

1 To hide or show the grid, choose View > Show / Hide Grid.

2 To create a ruler guide, first choose View > Show Rulers to display the rulers along the top and left edges of the image window. Position your cursor in a ruler and then click and drag onto your image to create either a vertical or horizontal guide.

3 To reposition a ruler guide, select the Move tool, position your cursor on a guide, then click and drag. The cursor changes to a bi-directional arrow when you pick up a guide.

4 To remove a ruler guide, drag the ruler guide back into the ruler it came from. Alternatively, choose View > Clear Guides to remove all guides.

Moving Around

Use any combination of the Navigator palette, the Zoom tool, the Hand tool and the scroll bars for moving around and zooming in and out of your image.

1 Choose Window > Show Navigator to show the Navigator palette. In the palette, you can double-click the % entry box, enter a zoom % (0.198 – 1600%), then press Return/Enter. Alternatively,

drag the zoom slider to the right to zoom in, or to the left to zoom out. Each time you change your zoom level, the view in the Proxy Preview area updates.

Hold down Command/Ctrl and the spacebar to temporarily access the zoom tool with any other tool selected. Add the Alt/Option key (Mac) or the Alt key (Windows) to the above combination to zoom out.

2 Drag the red box in the Proxy Preview area to move quickly to different areas of your image.

3 To use the Zoom tool, select it, position your cursor on the image and click to zoom in on the area around your cursor, in preset increments. With the Zoom tool selected, hold down alt/Alt. The cursor changes to the zoom out cursor; click to zoom out in the preset increments.

4 With the Zoom tool selected, you can also click and drag to define the area you want to zoom in on.

With any other tool selected, hold down the spacebar to temporarily access the hand tool.

5 You can use the Hand tool in addition to using the scroll bars to move around your image when you have zoomed in on it. Select the tool, position your cursor on the image, then click and drag to reposition.

The Info Palette

The Info palette (Window > Show Info) provides useful numerical read-outs relative to the position of the cursor on your image.

You can use it as an on-screen densitometer to examine colour values at the cursor. There are two colour read-outs. As a default, the first colour read-out is the actual colour under the cursor. For example, a read-out of red, green, and blue colour components in an RGB image. The default second read-out is for cyan, magenta, yellow and black values.

An exclamation mark next to the CMYK readouts indicates that a colour is out of gamut.

The palette also displays x and y coordinates, giving the precise location of the cursor as it moves over the image.

If you create a selection, there is a read-out of the width and height of the selection. The palette also displays values for some options such as rotating, skewing and scaling selections.

1 To change the default settings for the Info Palette, choose Palette Options from the pop-up menu.

2 Use the Mode pop-ups to choose the first and second colour read-outs.

3 You can also choose a unit of measurement for mouse coordinates.

Palette Techniques

There are eleven floating palettes in Photoshop. These movable palettes appear in front of images. Initially the palettes are grouped together. The default groupings for the palettes are Navigator-Info-Options, Colour-Swatches-Brushes, Layers-Channels-Paths-History-Actions.

1. You can show any of the palette groups by selecting the appropriate palette from the Window menu. To close a palette, click on the Close box (Mac) or Close icon (Windows) in the title bar of each palette.

This page uses Macintosh and Windows screen shots to illustrate the degree of similarity in functionality between the Windows and Macintosh platforms.

2. To move a palette, simply position your cursor in the title bar, then click and drag.

3. To choose a particular palette, click on the appropriate tab just below the title bar. You can drag these tabs to create separate palettes. Alternatively, you can drag a tab into another palette to create your own custom groupings of palettes.

4. You can shrink or roll up palettes to make the most of your available screen space. Click the Zoom box (Mac) or Minimise icon (Windows) in the title bar of the palette. Repeat the procedure to restore the palette to its original size. (You have to click twice on the Zoom/Minimise icon if the palette has been resized.)

5 You can use standard Macintosh and Windows techniques to resize the Swatches and Brushes, Navigator, Layers, Channels, Actions and Paths palettes by dragging.

6 You can collapse some of the palettes to show title bar and tabs only, by double-clicking a tab. Repeat the procedure to restore the palette to its original size.

7 Press the Tab key to hide/show all palettes including the toolbox. Hold down Shift, then press Tab to hide/show currently visible palettes, with the exception of the toolbox.

8 You can restore the default settings for a tool by choosing Reset Tool from the pop-up menu in the tool options palette. Choose Reset All Tools to restore default settings for all tools.

9 All palettes have a pop-up menu for accessing a range of commands or options relevant to the palette. Click the triangle to access the pop-up menu.

Saving and Loading Custom Settings

When you save settings, you are creating an independent file which stores the custom information.

The Swatches, Brushes and Actions palettes, along with dialogue boxes, such as Duotones, Levels and Curves, have Save and Load options which allow you to save custom settings made in the palette or dialogue box and then load them into the same image, or into other Photoshop images. The following example is for the Brushes palette.

1 When you have customised the Brushes palette (see pages 72–73 and 84), choose Save Brushes in the pop-up menu (in a dialogue box, click the Save button) to save the changes.

It's a good idea to set up a folder within your Adobe folder, or any other appropriate location, for saving your own custom settings. This means you will always be able to access and load the settings quickly and conveniently whenever you need them.

2 The Save Brushes In dialogue box prompts you for a file name and location in which to save the settings.

3 To load previously saved settings, choose Replace Brushes/Load Brushes in the pop-up (in a dialogue box click the Load Button), then specify the location of the settings you previously saved. Click on the name, then click Open. Load Brushes adds the new brushes to the existing brushes in the palette. Replace Brushes replaces the current brushes with the new set.

Look in the Goodies folder, within the Adobe folder, for palettes that come with Photoshop. Try the Assorted Brushes as a starting point for experimenting with brush types.

4 Choose Reset Brushes in the pop-up menu to restore settings to their original defaults.

Printing Composites – Mac

A composite image is an image which has not been colour separated and can be useful for low-cost, basic proofing purposes. In a black-and-white laser printer composite, you get a complete image on one sheet of paper, with all colour values converted to shades of grey.

The appearance of the Page Setup dialogue box varies according to the printer selected. Non-PostScript printers do not offer a complete set of options.

Page Setup

1 To print a composite image, first use the Chooser to select the printer you want to print to.

2 Choose File > Page Setup. Make sure the correct printer is selected from the 'Format for' pop-up. From the Paper pop-up, choose the actual physical size of the paper in your printer onto which you want to print. You can enter a Scale % entry box to increase/decrease the size of the image that prints. Use the Orientation buttons to control the orientation of the image.

3 Choose Adobe Photoshop from the pop-up to specify Photoshop print options. Click the Screen button to change the size, angle and shape of the halftone screen dots. This can be useful for creating special effects. Click the Transfer button to map brightness values in an image to different shades when printed. Background and Border are useful when printing slides. Use Bleed to print outside the 'imageable' area of the page when outputting to an imagesetter.

4 Choose PostScript Options from the pop-up to set further PostScript options if required.

Printing the image

Choose File > Image Info and enter a caption if you want a caption to print with the image.

1 Choose File > Print. With General selected, make sure you have the correct

printer chosen in the Printer pop-up. Enter the number of copies you want to print.

2 Choose Adobe Photoshop from the pop-up. Check that encoding is set to Binary. This is a more compact and quicker format for sending image data than ASCII. Make sure that Space is set to Greyscale. Click the Print button when you are satisfied with the settings.

Registration Marks

Centre Crop Marks

Corner Crop Marks

Calibration Bars

Printing Composites – Windows

A composite image is an image which has not been colour separated and can be useful for low-cost, basic proofing purposes. In a black and white laser printer composite, you get a complete image, with all colour values converted to shades of grey.

1 To print a composite proof, choose File > Page Setup. Select the printer you want to print to. Check that Paper Size and Orientation are correct. Click the check boxes for calibration bars and registration marks as required. OK the dialogue box.

You can choose File > Print, then click the Setup button to go into the Page Setup Dialogue box.

2 Choose File > Print. Select the Print As and Encoding options, then click OK. (Binary encoding is a quick, efficient method of encoding image data; ASCII encoding results in a larger, plain-text file, but offers greater compatibility when moving files to and from the Windows platform. JPEG can only be used with PostScript Level 2 printers.)

The History Palette

Every time you modify your image this is recorded in the History palette as a history state. The History palette records the last 20 states of the image.

Once you close an image, all recorded history states and snapshots are discarded.

Use the History palette to return to a previous state of the image within the current work session. The most recent state of the image appears at the bottom of the list in the palette. Each state indicates the name of the tool or command used on the image.

1 To return to a previous state of the image, make sure that the History palette is showing.

You can still use Edit > Undo to undo the last operation. In effect this steps you back one state in the History palette.

2 Click on a state in the History palette. The image reverts to that stage of the work session. States after the state you click on are dimmed. These subsequent states will be discarded if you continue to work from the selected state.

Use File > Revert to revert to the state of your image as it was when you last did a File > Save. The History palette is cleared of all previous history states when you use the Revert command.

3 Alternatively, drag the state slider up or down to indicate the state you wish to move to. Or, choose Step Forward/Step Backward from the pop-up menu in the History palette to move sequentially through the states. You can also use the keyboard shortcuts Command/Ctrl+Shift+Z to move to the next state. Use alt/Alt+Shift+Z to move to the previous state.

Deleting, Clearing & Purging States

There are three essential techniques for controlling the states listed in the History palette.

Deleting States

You can delete states from the History palette to remove the changes to the image recorded by that state and all subsequent states.

Both techniques for deleting states delete the selected state and all states that occur after it. In other words, you are reverting to the state of the image previous to the state you delete.

1   To delete a history state, click on the name of the state, then choose Delete from the pop-up menu in the History palette.

2   Alternatively, drag the state into the Wastebasket icon at the bottom of the palette.

Clearing States

Clearing states leaves the image at its current state, but removes all previous states from the History palette.

| To clear the History palette, use the pop-up menu to choose Clear History. All recorded states are deleted from the History palette, leaving the image at its most recent state.

Purging States

Purging states is useful if you get a low memory message. This is typically because the Undo buffer is becoming full with the changes to the image that it is having to record. When you purge states they are deleted from the Undo buffer, freeing up memory.

You cannot undo the Purge states commands.

| To purge states, hold down alt/Alt, then choose Clear History from the pop-up menu in the History palette. This command purges history states from the active image.

2   Choose Edit > Purge Histories if you want to purge all history states for all open images.

Taking Snapshots

By default the History palette records the result of the last 20 operations performed on an image. Older states of the image are automatically deleted. This keeps memory free for Photoshop. You can keep particular states of an image throughout a work session by taking a Snapshot of the image.

A Snapshot is created by default when you open an image. This appears at the top of the History palette.

| To create additional Snapshots, click on any state in the History palette.

2 Choose New Snapshot from the pop-up menu in the History palette. In the New Snapshot dialogue box enter a name. OK the dialogue box. A new Snapshot is added in the top section of the History palette.

Snapshots exist for the current work session only. When you close an image, all snapshots are lost.

Opening and Saving Files

Adobe Photoshop began life with the primary purpose of converting image formats for use on different applications and platforms. Since then it has gone on to become a market-leading image-editing application. This chapter covers the basic techniques of opening and saving images in Photoshop.

Covers

Opening Images in Photoshop | 40

Scanning into Photoshop | 41

Opening Photo CD Images | 42

Opening an EPS File | 43

Placing an EPS File | 45

Saving Files | 46

TIFF Format | 47

Photoshop EPS | 48

JPEG Format | 49

Creating a New File | 50

Chapter Three

Opening Images in Photoshop

Once you have launched Photoshop you can open images using the File menu. Some specialist file formats open using the File > Import command.

1   To open a picture from within Photoshop, choose File > Open. This takes you into the Open File dialogue box.

2   Navigate through folders and sub-folders as necessary to locate the file you wish to open, click on

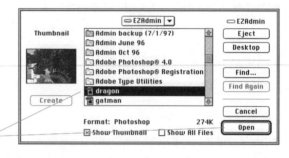

the file name to select it, then click Open. Alternatively, just double-click the file name.

Click the Create button if it is available for Photoshop to create a thumbnail preview of the file you have selected in the file list box.

3   Use the Show Thumbnail option either to hide or to show the thumbnail area to the left of the dialogue box. Select the Show All Files option (Mac), or choose All Formats from the

Files of Type pop-up (Windows), to show all files in the selected folder.

Double-click Photoshop file icons in the Windows or Macintosh file-management environments to open the file. If Photoshop is not running, this will also launch Photoshop.

4   In Windows you can use the Open As command to open a file that has a missing or incorrect file extension. You can also choose from a list of the most recently opened files at the bottom of the File menu.

Scanning into Photoshop

You can scan into Photoshop either using the TWAIN interface, using a scanner plug-in designed for use with Photoshop, or, if your scanner does not have a plug-in for Photoshop, you can use the scanner software to scan the image, save the image in TIFF, PICT or BMP format, then open the file in Photoshop.

Make sure the plug-in for your scanner is in Photoshop's Import/Export plug-ins folder. Plug-in modules for installed scanners appear in the File > Import submenu.

1   The first time you scan into Photoshop using the TWAIN interface, choose File > Import > TWAIN Select. Locate your scanner, select the scanner icon and click OK to specify the scanner.

2   Choose File > Import > TWAIN Acquire. This takes you into your scanning software.

```
Anti-aliased PICT...
PICT Resource...
Quick Edit...
Twain Acquire...
Twain Select...
```

Refer to your scanning software manual for details of the controls available. Typically, you can choose settings for scan mode (greyscale, colour, line art etc.), resolution, scale, contrast, brightness and gamma settings.

Many of the scanning controls have equivalent functions in Photoshop. Scanning options vary from scanner to scanner, but you should be able to specify whether you are scanning a transparency or a photograph. The other essential decisions you need to make at this stage are mode, resolution and scale. You will also need to specify a crop area in the preview window.

Mode:	Gray-Scale
Original:	Reflective
Output:	200 ppi
Scale To:	100%
Range:	Automatic
Tone Curve:	Gamma 1.8
Descreen:	None
Sharpness:	None
Preferences:	General
Settings:	Current

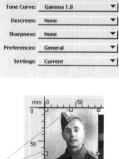

If your scanner does not have a plug-in for Photoshop, use the scanner software to scan the image, save the image in TIFF, PICT or BMP format, then open it in Photoshop.

3   Click the scan button. Wait until the scanning process finishes and the image appears in an untitled Photoshop window. Save the image.

Opening Photo CD Images

Photo CD files are found inside the Images folder within the Photo CD folder.

The Photo CD format, developed by Kodak, and using the YCC colour model, is becoming a more and more popular method for creating and storing digital images. The YCC colour model provides an extremely broad range of colour. The Kodak Precision Color Management System (KPCMS) lets you control the colour mode and display of Photo CD images by specifying profiles for the source film and the destination output device.

I   To open a Photo CD Image, choose File > Open. Select the image you want to open and click OK. The Photo CD Plug-in dialogue box appears.

The Kodak Precision Color Manage-ment System is automatically installed on your system when you install Photoshop.

2   Use the Resolution pop-up menu to choose a resolution from 128 x 192 pixels (72k, 2.667 by 1.778 inches) to 2,048 x 3,072 pixels (18Mb, 42.668 by 28.445 inches). In this case, resolution refers to the dimensions of the image in pixels. All Photo CD images open in Photoshop at a resolution of 72 pixels per inch.

3   Click the Image Info button. The dialogue box gives information about the image and the medium of the

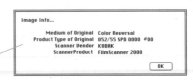

A product type of 052/55 denotes Universal Ektachrome, while 116/22 denotes Universal Kodachrome.

original. Make a note of the medium of the original – whether it was a colour negative or slide (Colour Reversal). For a Colour Reversal, make a note of the 'Product Type of Original'. You will use this information in the Source option to select the appropriate Precision Transform for a specific Photo CD image. OK the Image Info box.

Profiles are stored in System\ Preferences\ ColorSync Profiles folder (Mac); Windows\System \Colour folder (Windows). You may have to obtain the correct profiles before you can select them. (See page 15 for further information.)

4 Click the Source button. The folder in which ICC colour profiles are stored automatically opens. Make sure the Show Profile Attributes option is selected. Click on a profile to select it.

The attributes area at the bottom of the dialogue box will help you choose the correct profile according to the Product Type of Original you noted in the Image Info dialogue box. In this example the choice is Universal Ektachrome. If the Medium of Original is Colour Reversal, but you don't know the film type, use Universal Kodachrome. OK the dialogue box.

5 Click the Destination button. Select a profile for the output device. OK the dialogue box.

6 OK the Photo CD Plug-in dialogue box. The image will open in Photoshop.

Opening an EPS File

EPS files, which are created in applications such as Adobe Illustrator and Macromedia FreeHand, can contain object-oriented or 'vector' format information. When you open an EPS file in Photoshop, it is rasterized: that is, the vector information is converted into Photoshop's pixel-based format.

I To open an EPS file as a new document, choose File > Open. Locate and highlight an EPS picture to be opened, then click the Open button. Alternatively, double-click the file name.

2 In the Rasterize dialogue box, choose a unit of measurement from the pop-up menus next to the height and width fields, and enter new dimensions if required.

3 Enter the resolution required for your final output device and choose an image mode from the Mode pop-up menu.

4 Select the Constrain Proportions box to keep the original proportions of the EPS. Select Anti-aliased to slightly blur pixels along edges to avoid unwanted jagged edges.

5 Click OK. The EPS appears in its own image window. It is now a bitmap image.

Placing an EPS File

You can also 'place' an Illustrator or FreeHand EPS file into an open Photoshop document.

Before you place an EPS into Photoshop, it's a good idea to choose File > Preferences > General, then select the Anti-alias PostScript option. This preference helps create a smooth result.

1 To place an EPS file into an existing Photoshop file, first open a picture in Photoshop.

2 Choose File > Place. Use the Place Document dialogue box to specify the location and name of the EPS file, then click Place.

3 A bounding box with eight 'handles' and a cross through the placed image will appear on your Photoshop image. The EPS image itself may take a few seconds to draw inside the bounding box.

If you don't want to accept the placed image, with the bounding box still visible, press the Esc key. If you have already placed the image you will have to delete the new layer. (See page 116.)

4 Drag a corner handle to resize the placed image. Hold down Shift as you drag to maintain proportions. Position your cursor inside the bounding box of the placed image and drag to reposition the image.

5 When you are satisfied, press Return/ Enter, or double-click inside the bounding box. The rasterized file is placed on a new layer.

Saving Files

To create a thumbnail icon that will display in the thumbnail area of the Open dialogue box, choose File > Preferences > Saving Files. Select Always Save from the Image Previews pop-up, then click the Thumbnail option.

The basic principles of saving files in Photoshop – using 'Save' and 'Save As' – are the same as in any other Macintosh or Windows application. You should save regularly as you make changes to an image so that you do not lose changes you have made should a system crash occur. You should use Save As to save a new file in the first instance and to make copies of a file.

Photoshop supports numerous file formats for opening and saving images. Typically, you save an image in a particular format to meet specific output or printing specifications, to compress the image to save disk space, or to open or import the image into an application that requires a particular file format.

1 To save an image in the first instance, choose File > Save As. Specify where you want to save the file. Enter a name for the file. Use the Format pop-up to choose an appropriate format. Click the Save button. File extensions are added automatically.

To create image icons for the Finder on the Macintosh, choose File > Preferences > Saving Files. Select Always Save from the Image Previews pop-up, then click the Icon option.

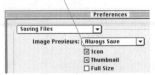

2 To save changes as you work on an image, choose File >Save. The previously saved file is updated.

Photoshop Format

Sometimes referred to as native format: use this format as you work on your image. Applications such as QuarkXPress will not import images in Photoshop format, but all of Photoshop's options, in particular layers, remain available to you when you save in this format. Photoshop also performs open and save routines more quickly when using its native format.

TIFF Format

TIFF (Tagged Image File Format), originally developed by Aldus, became a standard file format for scanned images in the early days of desktop publishing, and is common on both Mac and Windows platforms.

1 To save an image in TIFF format, choose File > Save As. The Save As dialogue box appears.

On the Macintosh, use the Saving Files preferences dialogue box to specify whether or not you want file extensions – e.g. '.tif – automatically added when saving files.

2 Specify where you want to save the image and enter a name in the name entry box. Use the Format pop-up menu to choose TIFF, then click OK.

3 The TIFF options dialogue box will appear. Select Byte Order options and LZW Compression as required, then OK the dialogue box.

Byte Order

Use this option to specify whether you want the TIFF to be used on a Mac or a PC, as Mac and PC TIFF formats vary slightly.

You can save clipping paths with images in TIFF file format.

LZW Compression

(Lempel-Ziv-Welch) is a compression format that looks for repeated elements in the computer code that describes the image and replaces these with shorter sequences. Most importantly, this is a 'lossless' compression scheme (i.e., none of the image's detail is lost). Applications such as QuarkXPress, Adobe PageMaker and Macromedia FreeHand can import TIFFs with LZW compression.

Photoshop EPS

EPS is generally more reliable for PostScript printing than TIFF file format, but generates file sizes which can be three to four times greater than TIFFs with LZW compression. To save in EPS format, do the following:

Follow the procedure for saving TIFFs, but choose Photoshop EPS from the Format pop-up menu. Click OK. The EPS format dialogue box will appear. Specify your settings, then click OK.

Preview

This option specifies the quality of the low-resolution screen preview you see when you import the image into applications such as Adobe PageMaker and QuarkXPress. Use 'Macintosh (8bits/pixel)' for a colour preview. 'Macintosh (JPEG)' uses JPEG compression routines, but is only supported by Postscript Level 2 printers. Use TIFF if you want to use the image in Windows.

Clipping paths saved with the image are automatically exported with the image when you choose Photoshop EPS file format.

Encoding

Use binary encoding if you want to export the image for use with Adobe Illustrator. Some applications do not recognise binary encoding; in this case you have to use ASCII.

JPEG Format

The JPEG compression routine is a 'lossy' procedure. To make the file size of the image smaller, image data is discarded, resulting in reduced image quality.

1. Follow the procedure for saving in TIFF format, but choose JPEG from the Format pop-up menu.

2. Use the Quality pop-up to specify the amount of compression, or drag the slider. Maximum gives best image quality, retaining most of the detail in an image, but results in the least compression. Low gives lowest image quality, but gives maximum compression.

3. In the Format Options area, select Baseline Optimised to optimise the colour quality of the image.

4. Select Progressive and enter a value for Scans if you intend to use the image on the World Wide Web and you want the image to download in a series of passes which add detail to the image progressively.

Format Options
○ Baseline ("Standard")
● Baseline Optimized
○ Progressive
Scans: 3 ▾

5. The compressed file size is indicated in the Size area. Choose a modem speed from the Size pop-up to see an estimated downlaod time for the image at the specified modem speed.

14.4Kbps
✓ 28.8Kbps
56.6Kbps

Creating a New File

When you need a fresh, completely blank canvas to work on, you can create a new file.

Whilst the New dialogue box is active, if you have an image window already open, you can choose the window's name from the bottom of the Window menu; the New dialogue box will update with the settings from the file you selected.

1 To create a new file, choose File > New. Enter a name for the new document (or leave this as Untitled and do a Save As later).

2 Specify width and height settings. If you have copied or cut pixels to the clipboard, the width and height fields automatically reflect the dimensions of the elements on the clipboard.

3 Enter a resolution and choose a colour mode.

4 Select one of the contents options to specify the canvas background you want to begin with, then OK the dialogue box.

You can also use the Fill command to fill selections with colour.

5 To change the colour of the canvas, select a foreground colour (see Chapter Five, 'Defining Colours'). Next, choose Edit > Fill. Choose Foreground from the Use pop-up. Make sure Opacity is set to 100% and Mode is Normal. Click OK.

Getting Started with Images

There are a number of common techniques and tasks, such as cropping an image and making it larger or smaller, or changing the resolution to suit your final output needs, that you need to undertake on many of the images on which you work. This chapter covers a range of these tasks.

Covers

Rotating an Image | 52

Resizing without Resampling | 53

Resampling Up | 54

Sampling Down | 56

Cropping an Image | 58

Adding a Border | 59

Image Modes | 60

Duotone Mode | 62

Chapter Four

Rotating an Image

You can quickly rotate an image if you have scanned it at the wrong orientation, or, for example, if you have opened a Photo CD image using the Landscape option.

To rotate an image in set increments, use Image > Rotate Canvas. Choose one of the preset increments. CW stands for clockwise, CCW for counter-clockwise. In the example above, you would choose 90 degrees counter-clockwise to rotate the Beijing Duck seller upright.

When using arbitrary rotation, position a ruler guide (see page 27, 'Ruler Guides and Grids') to help determine how far you need to rotate.

Sometimes you need to adjust an image a few degrees to make up for a poor original photograph or slightly misaligned scan:

2 To rotate in precise amounts, choose Image > Rotate Canvas > Arbitrary. Enter a value for the rotation. Choose the clockwise or counter-clockwise radio button, then OK the dialogue box.

3 You may need to recrop the image. Use Unsharp mask to compensate for any blurring due to the rotation.

Resizing without Resampling

When you make the image smaller without resampling, the pixels get smaller. Effectively, you are increasing the resolution of the image. When you make an image bigger without resampling, the pixels get larger and this can lead to jagged, blocky results. Effectively, you are reducing the resolution of the image.

When you resize an image without resampling, you make the image larger or smaller without changing the total number of pixels in the image. The overall dimensions of the image change, the file size remains the same, but the resolution of the image goes up if you make the image smaller, down if you make the image larger.

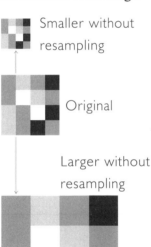

Smaller without resampling

Original

Larger without resampling

1 To decrease the size of your image without resampling, choose Image > Image Size. Make sure that Resample Image is deselected. Enter a lower value in the Width or Height entry box. The other measurement updates automatically. The file size of the image remains the same – no pixels have been added. The resolution has increased – the same number of pixels are packed into a smaller area.

2 To increase the size of your image without resampling, enter a higher value in the Width or Height entry box. The file size of the image remains the same, but the resolution has decreased.

Resampling Up

Resampling up involves interpolation. Interpolation is used when Photoshop has to add information – new pixels – that didn't previously exist to an image. There are three methods to choose from the pop-up in the Image size dialogue box. Bicubic gives best results, but takes longest; Nearest Neighbour is quickest, but least accurate.

When you resample up, new pixels are added to the image, so file size increases. Resampling takes place when you increase the resolution setting, or the width/height setting with the Resample Image option selected.

This example starts with a 2 in by 2 in image at 72 ppi.

1 Choose Image > Image Size. To keep the overall dimensions of the image, but increase the resolution, make sure that Resample Image is selected. Select Constrain Proportions so that the image's original proportions are maintained. Enter a higher value in the Resolution box.

To reset the dialogue box to its original settings, hold down alt/Alt, then click the Reset button.

2 The file size and total number of pixels increase, but the width and height dimensions remain the same.

You now have an image which is the same overall size, but which has more pixels in the same area, and therefore its resolution is increased:

When you resample an image, blurring may occur due to the process of interpolation. Use the Unsharp Mask filter to compensate for this. (See pages 177–178.)

3 To make the overall dimensions of the image bigger, but to keep the same resolution, again make sure that Resample Image is selected. Select Constrain Proportions to keep width and height proportional. Enter a higher value in either the Width or Height entry boxes. (The other entry box will update automatically if you have selected Constrain Proportions.)

4 The overall dimensions of the image have now increased. The file size and total number of pixels have also increased, but the resolution remains the same.

Sampling Down

You sometimes need to resample down to maintain an optimal balance between the resolution needed for acceptable final output and file size considerations. There is little point in working with an image at too high a resolution if some of the image information is redundant at final output.

Resampling down means discarding pixels. The result is a smaller file size. Resampling down occurs when you decrease the resolution setting, or the width/ height setting with Resample Image option selected.

These examples start with a 2 by 2 inch image at 300 ppi.

1 Choose Image > Image Size. To keep the overall dimensions of the image, but decrease the resolution, make sure that Resample Image is selected. Leave Constrain Proportions selected, so that the image's original proportions are maintained. Reduce the value in the Resolution box.

2 The file size goes down and the total number of pixels decreases, whilst the width and height dimensions remain the same.

You now have an image which is the same overall size, but with fewer pixels in the same area, and therefore its resolution is decreased:

3 To reduce the overall dimensions of the image, but keep the image at the same resolution, again make sure that Resample Image is selected. (Select Constrain Proportions to keep the width and height proportional.) Enter a lower value in either the width or height entry box. (The other entry box will update automatically if you have selected Constrain Proportions.)

4 The overall dimensions of the image have now decreased. The file size and the total number of pixels have also decreased, but the resolution remains the same.

Cropping an Image

Use the Crop tool to crop unwanted areas of an image and reduce the file size.

Press C on the keyboard to select the Crop tool, then press Return/Enter to show the Crop tool options palette.

1 Select the Crop tool from the Marquee group. You can double-click the tool to show the Crop tool options palette.

2 Position your cursor on the image, then click and drag to define the crop area. Don't worry if you don't get the crop exactly right first time.

Hold down Shift, then click and drag on a corner handle to resize the crop marquee in proportion.

3 • To reposition the crop marquee, place your cursor inside the marquee, then click and drag.

• To resize the crop marquee, place your cursor on one of the 8 handles around the marquee (the cursor changes to a bi-directional arrow), then click and drag.

The Crop tool snaps to the edge of the image. To prevent the snap effect, hold down Command/Ctrl as you create or resize the crop marquee.

• To rotate the marquee, position your cursor just outside the marquee (the cursor changes shape to indicate rotation), then click and drag in a circular direction.

4 When you are satisfied with the position and size of the crop marquee, press Return/Enter to crop the picture. Alternatively, you can double-click inside the crop marquee. The areas outside the marquee are discarded. Press the Esc key if you do not want to accept the crop marquee.

Adding a Border

Borders are useful when you need additional space around the edges of your image.

Make sure that you select a background colour for your border, before you use the Canvas Size dialogue box.

1 Choose Image > Canvas Size. Use the measurement pop-up menus to choose a unit of measurement. Enter increased values for the width and/or height fields.

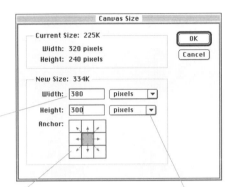

2 To specify where the border is added relative to the image, click one of the white placement squares. This sets the relative position of the image and the border. The grey square represents the position of the image, the white squares the position of the border.

3 OK the dialogue and the border is added, filled with the background colour.

Image Modes

Bitmap
Grayscale
Duotone
Indexed Color...
✓RGB Color
CMYK Color
Lab Color
Multichannel

✓8 Bits/Channel
16 Bits/Channel

Color Table...

Image modes are fundamental to working in Photoshop. When you open an image the mode is indicated in the title bar of the image window. There are eight different modes in Photoshop. Use modes as appropriate to your working requirements. Then, depending on output or printing requirements, if necessary, convert to a different mode.

RGB Mode

Images are typically scanned or captured in RGB mode. When you start work with a colour image it is usually best to work in RGB mode, as this is faster than CMYK mode and allows you to use all of Photoshop's commands and features, providing greatest flexibility.

The disadvantage of working in RGB mode, if your image will be printed, is that RGB allows a greater gamut of colours than you can print. At some stage, some of the brightest, most vibrant colours may lose their brilliance when the image is brought within the CMYK gamut.

CMYK Mode

Convert to CMYK when the image is to be printed and you have finished making changes.

You can retain the flexibility of working in RGB mode, but see an on-screen CMYK preview of your image, by choosing View > CMYK Preview. (You may have to wait a few seconds when you choose this option as Photoshop builds its colour conversion tables.)

To place a colour image in a page layout application from where it will be colour separated, you need to convert from RGB to CMYK. When you convert from RGB to CMYK, Photoshop adjusts any colours in the RGB image that fall outside the CMYK gamut to their nearest printable colour. (See Chapter Five, 'Defining Colours', for details on gamut warnings.)

You can also select Display out of Gamut colours from the View menu, to highlight (in grey) areas of the image that are out of gamut.

Indexed Colour Mode

This mode reduces your image to 256 colours or less and is frequently used for multimedia and Web images. (See Chapter 15, 'Web and Multimedia Images'.)

You must first convert to greyscale mode before you can convert to Duotone mode.

Duotone

For details on using Duotone mode see the following page.

Greyscale Mode

When you are not printing an image in colour you can convert to greyscale mode to make working faster and file size smaller.

Lab Mode

This mode uses the CIE Lab mode which has one channel for luminosity, an 'a' channel representing colours blue to yellow, a 'b' channel for magenta to green. A significant advantage to this mode is that its gamut encompasses that of both CMYK and RGB modes.

Bitmap Mode

This mode reduces everything to black or white pixels. The image becomes a one-bit image.

To convert from one mode to another, choose Image > Mode and choose the mode you want from the submenu. Depending on which mode you are converting from and to, you may get a message box warning you of any consequences of converting to the new mode and asking you to confirm your request.

Duotone Mode

You can only access Duotone mode when you have converted to Greyscale mode.

Duotone is a very popular effect used to give added tonal depth to a greyscale image by printing with black and another colour.

1 To create a duotone, choose Image > Mode > Duotone. Choose from the pop-up whether you want to create a duotone (two inks), a tritone (three inks) or a quadtone (four inks).

When you start working with Photoshop, click on the Load button and try using one of the preset duotone settings that can be found in: Adobe Photoshop > Goodies > Adobe Photoshop Only > Duotone Presets > Duotones.

2 To choose a second colour for the duotone, click the 'Ink 2' colour box (below the black ink box). This takes you into the Custom Colours dialogue box. Choose a colour. Click the Picker button if you want to use the Colour Picker. OK the dialogue box.

3 To specify the ink coverage for both colours, click on first the Ink 1 Curve box, then the Ink 2 box. In the Duotone Curve dialogue box. Drag the curve to the desired position, or enter values in the % entry boxes to adjust the ink coverage curve. Click the Preview option to preview the result in the image window before you OK the dialogue boxes.

Make sure you save duotones in EPS format so that they colour separate correctly from page layout applications.

Defining Colours

Defining colours is an essential aspect of using Photoshop and there is a range of techniques that can be used. The colour controls in the Toolbox indicate the current foreground and background colours.

Covers

Foreground and Background Colours | 64

The Eyedropper and Colour Sampler Tools (I) | 65

The Colour Picker Palette | 66

Selecting Pantone Colours | 68

The Colour Palette | 69

The Swatches Palette | 70

Chapter Five

Foreground and Background Colours

The foreground colour is applied when you create type, and when you use the Paint Bucket, Line, Pencil, Airbrush and Paintbrush tools.

The background colour is the colour you erase to when you use the Eraser tool, or when you delete or move a selection.

When you are working with foreground and background controls you can also switch colours, and you can quickly change back to the default colours, black and white.

You can change the background and foreground colours using the Eyedropper tool, the Colour Picker palette, the Colour palette and the Swatches palette.

Press X on the keyboard to switch background and foreground colours. Press D on the keyboard to revert to the default foreground and background colours.

1 To switch background to foreground and vice versa, click once on the Switch Colours arrow.

2 To revert to black and white as the default background and foreground colours, click the Default colours icon.

The Eyedropper and Colour Sampler Tools (I)

The Eyedropper Tool

The Eyedropper tool provides a quick and convenient way to pick up foreground and background colour from an area of the image you are working on, or from another inactive Photoshop image window.

1 To set the foreground colour, click on the Eyedropper tool.

2 Position your cursor, then click once on the image. (The foreground box in the Toolbox now represents the colour where you clicked.)

You can use the Eyedropper Options palette to specify the sample area of the image that the Eyedropper picks up. (Double-click the Eyedropper tool to show the Eyedropper Options palette if it is not already showing.)

3 To set the background colour, hold down alt/Alt, then click on the image. The background box in the Toolbox now indicates the colour on which you clicked.

4 To set the Sample Size, use the Sample Size pop-up menu to choose a value. Point Sample reads the precise value of the pixel on which you click. 3 by 3 and 5 by 5 take average values of the pixels where you click.

The Colour Sampler Tool

Use the Colour Sampler tool, in conjunction with the Info palette, to set up to four sample points, which you can refer to as you make adjustments to colour values in the image. Each time you click in the image window with the Colour Sampler tool, you set a sample point. Each sample point you set creates an extra pane in the Info palette. To delete a sample point, drag it out of the image window using the Colour Sampler tool.

To hide/show the sample points, choose Hide/Show Sample Points from the Info palette pop-up.

The Colour Picker Palette

One of the most powerful and flexible ways of choosing foreground and background colours is using the Colour Picker palette. You can use a number of different colour models to create colour.

Press the Tab key to move the highlight through the entry boxes in the dialogue box.

1 To create a Process colour using the Colour Picker, click once on either the foreground or background colour box.

A warning triangle – the Gamut alarm – will appear next to the Current/ Previous colour boxes if you create a colour that cannot be printed using CMYK inks. Click the warning triangle to choose the nearest printable colour. The small box below the warning triangle indicates the nearest printable colour.

2 Enter values in the CMYK entry boxes. You will see a preview of the colour in the Current Colour swatch, above the Previous Colour swatch.

3 OK the dialogue box. The colour you defined now becomes the foreground or background colour, depending on which box you clicked in step 1.

You can also create colours using the Colour Slider and the Colour field. The next example looks at creating a colour using Hue, Saturation and Brightness values. You can apply the same techniques to Red, Green, Blue (RGB) and Lab colour models.

1 To create a colour using Hue, Saturation and Brightness (HSB) values, first click the Hue radio button.

2 Click on the Colour Slider bar, or drag the slider triangles on either side of the bar, to choose a hue or colour. This sets

one of the three HSB values. The number in the Hue entry box represents the hue you have chosen (0–360).

3   Next, click in the Colour Field to set the other two variables – Saturation and Brightness. Clicking to the left of the field reduces the saturation, clicking to the right increases the saturation of the selected hue. Clicking near the bottom decreases brightness, clicking near the top increases brightness for the selected hue.

4   If you click on the Saturation button, the Colour Slider now represents saturation (from 0–100) and the colour field allows you to choose Hue and Brightness values. When you click the Brightness radio button, the slider represents Brightness and the colour field represents Hue and Saturation.

If the Web Colours Only option is deselected, the Non-web colour alert appears if you create a colour that is not in the Web palette.

Web-safe Colours

To create a Web-safe colour, select the Only Web Colours option. Fewer colours are represented in the Colour Field; each colour exists in the Web palette which consists of 216 colours.

Selecting Pantone Colours

You can access a range of colour-matching systems using the Colour Picker dialogue box. These include: Toyo Colour Finder 1050 System, Focoltone Colour System, Pantone Matching System, Trumatch Swatching System and DIC Colour Guide. Here, we'll select a Pantone colour.

1 To select a Pantone colour, click the foreground or background colour box. The Colour Picker dialogue box will appear. Click the Custom button.

2 Use the Book pop-up menu to select a Pantone matching system.

3 If you know the Pantone number of the colour you want, you can enter the number on the keyboard. Alternatively, click in the colour slider bar to the right of the Pantone colour boxes.

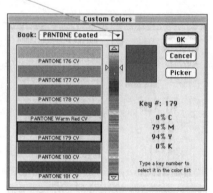

This moves you to a general range of colours. Then click on the scroll bars at the top and bottom of the sliders to find the specific Pantone colour you want.

4 Click on the colour you want to select, then click OK.

The Colour Palette

You can also use the Colour palette (Window > Show Colours) to mix new colours.

1 First identify which colour selection box is 'active'. There are two boxes, foreground and background. The active box is outlined in black.

2 Continue with step 3 if the correct box is active, or click the inactive box to make it the active box if necessary.

3 Drag the colour slider triangles below the colour slider bars, or enter values in the entry boxes to the right of the palette. You can also click on a colour in the Colour Bar running along the bottom of the Colour palette. The Colour Bar contains every colour in the CMYK spectrum as a default setting.

4 Use the pop-up triangle in the top right of the palette to change the colour model for sliders.

5 Choose an option from the bottom half of the pop-up menu to specify the colour model for the colours in the Colour Bar at the bottom of the Colour palette.

The Swatches Palette

You can use the Swatches palette (Window > Show Swatches) to set foreground and background colours, and you can also use it to create custom palettes which you can save and then reload into a different image.

See page 32 for details on loading and saving custom palette settings.

1 To select a foreground colour from the Swatches palette, click on a colour swatch.

2 To select a background colour, hold down alt/Alt and then click on a colour swatch.

You can customise the Swatches palette by adding and deleting colours in the palette.

Shift-clicking on an existing swatch replaces it with the current foreground colour. Pressing Shift and then alt/Alt while clicking on a swatch inserts the current foreground colour to the left of the colour you click.

3 To add colour to the swatches, select a foreground colour. Position your cursor in an empty area of the Swatches palette. (The cursor changes to a paint bucket.) Then click to add the current foreground colour to the Swatches palette.

4 To delete a colour swatch, hold down Command (Mac) or Ctrl (Windows) and then click on a colour swatch.

The Painting Tools

The Paintbrush, Airbrush, Pencil, and Line tools apply the foreground colour to pixels in your image as you drag across them. Each painting tool creates a painting stroke with different characteristics. You can use the Brushes palette to determine the shape, size and type of the brush stroke for the Airbrush, Paintbrush, and Pencil tools.

All the painting and editing tools can be used within a selection or directly on an image.

Covers

The Brushes Palette | 72

Painting Tool Techniques and Settings | 74

The Paintbrush Tool (B) | 76

The Airbrush Tool (J) | 77

The Pencil and Line Tools (N) | 78

The Gradient Tool (G) | 80

The Paint Bucket Tool (K) | 81

Blending Modes | 82

Defining a Brush | 84

Chapter Six

The Brushes Palette

The Brushes palette is central to using the painting and editing tools. Before you use any of these tools you need to check your brush size and shape. Choose Window > Show Brushes to show the Brushes palette.

1 To choose a hard-edged brush, click a brush in the first row of the default palette. To use a soft-edged brush, click one of the brushes in the second row. (The circle icons in the first two rows represent the actual size of the brush.) The third row contains brushes that are too large to be represented at their actual size. The number below them is the diameter of the brush in pixels. The remaining brushes create more painterly brush strokes.

You can use Brush Options from the pop-up menu to edit the settings for a selected brush.

2 To create a new brush, choose New Brush from the pop-up menu. Enter values for Diameter, Hardness, Spacing, Angle and Roundness in the New Brush dialogue box.

Diameter

Enter a value in pixels for the diameter of your brush from 1–999. Brush sizes too large to be represented at their actual size will display with the diameter indicated as a number.

Hardness

A setting of 100% gives a hard-edged brush. Settings below 100% produce soft-edged brushes. The lower you take this setting, the more diffuse the resultant stroke when you paint with the brush. Even with a setting of 100%, the edge of the brush-stroke is anti-aliased.

Spacing

Spacing is measured as a percentage of brush size. 25% is the default setting for all brushes. Higher settings begin to create non-continuous strokes.

Angle and Roundness

Use these controls together to create a stroke which thickens and thins like a calligraphic pen. You can enter values in the entry boxes, or drag the arrow indicator to change the angle, and drag the diameter dots to change the diameter.

3 OK the dialogue box. The new brush is added to the palette. The keyline around it indicates that it is selected. (See page 32 for details on saving customised palettes for future use.)

 To delete a brush, click on it to select it, then choose Delete brush in the pop-up menu.

Painting Tool Techniques and Settings

Each painting tool has its own Options palette. There is a range of Options palette settings and techniques common to many of the painting and editing tools. Use the options covered here in conjunction with the specific controls for each of the tools on the following pages.

With a tool selected, press Return/Enter to show its Options palette.

Opacity, Pressure and Exposure

Opacity (Paintbrush, Line, Pencil, Eraser, Rubber Stamp), Pressure (Airbrush, Smudge, Focus tools) and Exposure (Toning tools) have a similar effect and determine the intensity of the tool you are working with. For example, opacity controls how completely pixels are covered by the foreground colour when you drag across them.

Make sure the Opacity/Pressure slider is at 100% if you want to completely cover the pixels you drag across. (Soft-edged brushes only partially cover pixels around the edge of the painting stroke to create the soft edge effect.) Reducing the Opacity/Pressure setting gives less complete results in the area you drag across, creating a semi-transparent, partially-covered effect.

Number keys on the keyboard can be used to set Opacity. With a painting tool selected, type two numbers in quick succession to specify Opacity settings.

Fade

Use the Fade setting to create the effect of paint on the painting tool running out as you drag across the image. The rate of Fade controls the number of pixels that are coloured before the paint fades to nothing. The higher the Fade setting, the further the paint goes before it fades out completely.

1 To set a fade rate for the Paintbrush, Airbrush or Pencil, double-click the tool to show the tool's Options palette.

2 Enter a fade value and use the Transparency/Background pop-up to specify what you want to fade to.

Fade: 20	steps to	Transparent ▾
Stylus Pressure: ☐ Size		• Transparent
		Background

Undoing

To undo the last stroke you painted, choose Edit > Undo. This only works for the very last action you performed. In instances where you need to undo several steps, you can use the History palette. Use File > Revert to revert to the version of the file when you last saved it.

Cursor Types

Press Caps Lock to change painting and editing tool cursors to precise crosshairs. This is a very useful technique for making fine adjustments.

Whilst you are working with a painting tool, hold down alt/ Alt to temporarily access the Eyedropper tool. This is useful for selecting a new foreground colour with which to paint.

2 Choose File > Preferences > Display and Cursors to change the way your painting tool cursors appear on-screen. 'Precise' has the same effect as pressing Caps Lock. 'Brush Size' is useful because you see the actual brush size represented on screen. (Changing the Painting Cursors preference to Precise reverses the effect of Caps Lock.)

Painting Tool Options Palettes

You can use the pop-up menu in each of the painting tool Options palettes to reset the default setting for the tool, or you can reset defaults for all tools.

The Paintbrush Tool (B)

The Paintbrush in Photoshop is like a normal paintbrush. You drag it across the pixels in your image and it colours those pixels with the foreground colour.

You can use a Fade setting to make the paint run out, just as with a normal paintbrush. You can also change the opacity setting to achieve a translucent, partial coverage of the pixels you drag across.

Remember to choose an appropriate brush size and shape before you begin painting.

1 To paint with the Paintbrush, Line, Pencil or Airbrush, first double-click the tool to show the Options palette for that tool if it is not already showing.

2 Choose the settings you want, then position your cursor on the image, click and drag.

To constrain your painting strokes to straight lines, click with the painting tool to position the start of the stroke, move your cursor, (do not click and drag), then hold down Shift and click to end the stroke.

Wet Edges (Paintbrush & Eraser)

When you paint with wet edges selected you get a stroke that is darker around the edges and translucent inside the stroke, imitating the uneven build-up of paint in a watercolour.

Standard   Wet Edges

Fade = 60

The Airbrush Tool (J)

Use the Airbrush tool to imitate the effect of spraying paint with an airbrush. The airbrush paints with the foreground colour.

I To paint with the Airbrush tool, double-click the Airbrush tool to display the Airbrush Options palette if it is not already showing. Use the palette to specify the settings for: Blending Mode, Pressure and Fade.

Use the Brushes palette to specify an Airbrush size and shape. Use a soft-edged brush to create the most realistic airbrush effect.

2 Click and drag across the image to apply the foreground colour. The more you spray over an area, the greater the build-up of colour. The speed at which you drag the airbrush also affects the intensity of the paint.

For a description of Blending modes see pages 82–83.

To change the Pressure setting using the keyboard, type numbers on the keyboard. For example, type 70 to specify a Pressure setting of 70%.

The Pencil and Line Tools (N)

The Pencil Tool

You can use the Pencil tool to draw
freeform lines. The lines you draw with
the Pencil tool are always hard-edged – in
other words, the edges of your lines are
not anti-aliased. The Pencil tool paints or
draws with the foreground colour.

1 To draw a line, double-click the Pencil tool to show the
Pencil Tool Options palette if it is not already showing. Use
the Pencil Options palette to specify: Blending Mode,
Opacity, Fade and Auto Erase options.

*Use the
Brushes palette
to specify the
size of your
pencil.*

2 Click and drag to create a freeform pencil stroke. Click, hold
down Shift, then drag to constrain the pencil stroke vertically
or horizontally. Click, move the cursor to a new position (do
not click and drag), hold down Shift, then click again to
create a straight pencil stroke between the two points.

Auto Erase

Select this option to use the Pencil tool as an eraser.

The Line Tool

Use the Line tool to create straight lines. Lines are filled with the foreground colour. Lines are always hard-edged.

You cannot specify a brush size for the Line tool; use the Line Width setting in the Line Tool Options palette instead.

1 To draw a straight line, double-click the Line tool to show the Line Tool Options palette. Use the palette to specify Mode, Opacity and Line Width as desired.

2 Click and drag on the image to create a line. You can hold down Shift as you click and drag to constrain the line to 45-degree increments.

You must specify arrowhead settings before you create a line.

3 To add arrowheads to the beginning or end of a line, click the Start/End options as appropriate. Click the Shape button to define the shape of the arrowhead.

4 Enter Width, Length and Concavity settings. OK the dialogue box, then click and drag to create the line.

Length

Width   Concavity

Width = 300, Length = 600, Concavity = 0

Width = 300, Length = 250, Concavity = 0

Width = 300, Length = 600, Concavity = 20

The Gradient Tool (G)

You can use the Gradient tools to create transitions from one colour to another. You can also create multi-coloured gradients. There are tools for Linear, Radial, Angle, Reflected and Diamond gradients. You can apply a gradient fill to a selection, or to an entire active layer.

I   To create a gradient fill, choose one of the Gradient tools and double-click the tool to show the Gradient Tool Options palette if it is not already showing.

2   Select a Blending mode and set Opacity. Use the gradient pop-up to choose from one of the preset gradients.

Hold down Shift as you click and drag to constrain a linear gradient to 45-degree increments.

3   Position your cursor where you want the gradient to start, then click and drag. The angle and distance you drag the cursor defines the angle and distance of a linear gradient, or the radius of a radial gradient. (Click and drag from the centre out to create Radial, Angle, Reflected and Diamond gradient fills.)

4   For basic gradient fills leave the Transparency and Dither options selected.

For a linear gradient, the start and end colours fill any part of the selection that you do not drag the cursor across. For radial gradients, the end colour fills the remaining area.

Linear

Radial

Angle

Reflected

Diamond

The Paint Bucket Tool (K)

You can use the Paint Bucket tool to colour pixels with the foreground colour, based on a tolerance setting. It works in a similar way to the Magic Wand tool, but in this case, filling adjoining pixels that fall within the tolerance setting. You can use the Paint Bucket tool within a selection or on the entire image.

1 To fill an area with the foreground colour, double-click the Paint Bucket tool to show the Paint Bucket Options palette if it is not already showing. Enter a value from 0–255 in the Tolerance box. The higher you set the value, the greater the range of pixels the Paint Bucket will fill.

The Anti-aliased option creates a slightly soft edge on the areas that the Paint Bucket fills.

2 Set Opacity, Blending mode, Anti-aliased and Sample Merged options. Position your cursor then click on the image.

3 You can use the Paint Bucket to fill with a pattern previously saved into the pattern buffer. Use the Contents pop-up to specify whether the Paint Bucket fills with the foreground colour or a pattern.

You cannot use the Paint Bucket on images in Bitmap mode.

4 Deselect the Contiguous option to allow the Paint Bucket pixels anywhere in the image, provided that they fall within the Tolerance setting.

Blending Modes

The blending modes allow you to make changes to an image using the painting and editing tools in a more selective and subtle way than simply painting with the foreground colour. The colour you paint with (the blend colour) combines with the colour of the pixels you drag across (the base colour) to produce a different colour depending on the blending mode you select.

Choose blending modes from the pop-up menu in the Painting Tool Options palettes. The various paint modes in combination with opacity/pressure settings have a selective control on which pixels are affected when you use the painting and editing tools. The result is more of a blending of the paint colour and the colour of the base pixels than simply one colour replacing another.

• Normal
Dissolve
Behind
Multiply
Screen
Overlay
Soft Light
Hard Light
Color Dodge
Color Burn
Darken
Lighten
Difference
Exclusion
Hue
Saturation
Color
Luminosity

Dissolve

Produces a grainy, chalk-like effect. Not all pixels are coloured as you drag across the image, leaving gaps and holes in the stroke. Use Opacity to control the effect.

Behind

Only available when you are working on a layer with a transparent background. Use Behind to paint behind the existing pixels on a layer. Paint appears in the transparent areas, but does not affect the existing pixels.

Multiply

Combines the colour you are painting with the colour of the pixels you drag across, to produce a colour that is darker than the original colours.

Screen

Produces the opposite effect to Multiply. It multiplies the opposite of the original colour by the painting colour and has the effect of lightening the pixels.

Overlay

This increases the contrast and saturation, combining foreground colour with the pixels you drag across.

Soft Light

Creates a soft lighting effect. Lightens colours if the painting colour is lighter than 50% grey, darkens colours if the painting colour is darker than 50% grey.

Blending modes are also available in the Layers palette and in the Fill Path, Fill, Stroke and Fade dialogue boxes.

Use the Opacity/ Pressure setting to control the intensity of the effect.

Be prepared to experiment with blending modes to fully understand their results and to get the best out of them.

Hard Light

Multiplies or screens pixels, depending on the paint colour, and tends to increase contrast.

Darken

Applies the paint colour to pixels that are lighter than the paint colour – doesn't change pixels darker than the paint colour.

Lighten

Replaces pixels darker than the paint colour, but does not change pixels lighter than the paint colour.

Difference

It looks at the brightness of pixels and the paint colour, then subtracts paint brightness from pixel brightness. Depending on the result, it inverts the pixels.

Exclusion

The result is similar to Difference, but with lower contrast.

Hue

In colour images, applies the hue (colour) of the paint, without affecting the saturation or luminosity of the base pixels.

Saturation

Changes the saturation of pixels based on the saturation of the blend colour, but does not affect hue or luminosity.

Luminosity

Changes the relative lightness or darkness of the pixels without affecting their hue or saturation.

Colour

Applies the hue and saturation of the blend colour, but does not affect the luminosity of the base pixels.

Colour Dodge

Lightens the base colour – more pronounced when the paint colour is light.

Colour Burn

Darkens the base colour – more pronounced when paint colour is dark.

Defining a Brush

You can create your own custom brush strokes from
selections.

1 To create a brushstroke, make
a selection, then choose Define
Brush from the pop-up menu in
the Brushes palette.
The new brush is
added to the Brushes
palette.

2 Double-click the brush if you
want to change the spacing and
anti-aliased options. Anti-aliased
is not available for very large
brush sizes.

3 You can then use a painting tool to paint with the new
brush. In this example a fade of 30 has been set.

The Editing Tools

The editing tools – Blur and Sharpen, Smudge, Rubber and Pattern Stamp, Dodge, Burn, Sponge and Eraser – allow you to edit or change pixels in a variety of ways.

The editing tools can be used within a selection or anywhere on an image. Use the Brushes palette to specify a brush size for the editing tool. Many of the techniques and keyboard shortcuts covered for the painting tools apply to the editing tools as well.

Covers

The Blur, Sharpen and Smudge Tools (R) | 86

The Rubber and Pattern Stamp Tools (S) | 88

The Dodge, Burn and Sponge Tools (O) | 90

The Eraser Tool (E) | 92

The Magic Eraser Tool (E) | 93

The Background Eraser Tool (E) | 95

Chapter Seven

The Blur, Sharpen and Smudge Tools (R)

The Blur Tool

The Blur and Sharpen tools are the two 'Focus' tools. The Blur tool works by reducing contrast between pixels and can be useful for disguising unwanted, jagged edges and softening edges between shapes.

Remember to set an appropriate brush size before you start working with the Blur/ Sharpen tool.

| To blur areas of your image, select the Blur tool. If the Blur Options palette is not showing, you can double-click the Blur tool to show it.

You cannot use the Blur/ Sharpen tool on an image in bitmap or indexed colour mode.

2 Set the Blend (Effect) mode, Pressure and Use All Layers options, position your cursor on the image, then click and drag to blur the pixels. Release the mouse then drag across the pixels again to intensify the effect.

The Sharpen Tool

The Sharpen tool works by increasing the contrast between pixels.

| To sharpen areas of an image, select the Sharpen tool. Double-click the Sharpen tool to show the Sharpen Options palette.

Each Focus tool retains its own settings when you switch to the other tool.

2 Position your cursor, then click and drag to sharpen the pixels. Click and drag across the same area of the image again, to intensify the sharpening effect. You will produce a coarse, grainy effect if you overuse the Sharpen tool. Use a low pressure setting and build up the effect gradually.

The Smudge Tool

You can use the Smudge tool to create an effect similar to dragging your finger through wet paint. The Smudge tool picks up colour from where you start to drag and smears it into adjacent colours.

Hold down alt/ Alt to temporarily turn Finger Painting on or off, depending on whether the option is selected in the Options palette.

1 Double-click the Smudge tool to show the Smudge Tool Options palette if it is not already showing. Set the pressure, position your cursor on the image, then start to drag across your image to smudge the colours. The higher the pressure setting, the more pronounced the effect.

2 Select the Finger Painting option if you want to begin the smudge with the current foreground colour.

3 Select the Use All Layers option if you want to smudge colours from other layers in the image onto the layer you are working on. Leave this option deselected if you want the smudge to pick up colour from pixels on the active or target layer only.

Use All Layers

Select this option when you want Photoshop to take into account, or 'sample', pixels from layers other than the target layer. In other words, it samples from layers as if they were merged.

The Rubber and Pattern Stamp Tools (S)

You can use the Rubber Stamp tool to retouch your image by cloning or duplicating areas of your image. This is very useful when you want to remove blemishes and scratches from images. Use the Pattern Stamp tool to paint with a predefined pattern.

The Rubber Stamp Tool

1 To clone an area of your image, double-click the Rubber Stamp tool to show the Rubber Stamp Options palette if it is not already showing. Remember to set an appropriate brush size.

2 Make sure that the Aligned option is selected. Hold down alt/Alt and click on the part of the image you want to clone.

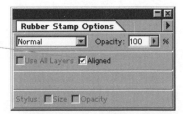

3 Release alt/Alt. Move your cursor to a different part of your image, then click and drag. The pixels in the image where you drag are replaced by pixels cloned from the spot where you first clicked. A crosshair at the point where you first clicked indicates the pixels that are being cloned – the source point.

Clone – Aligned

With the Aligned option selected, the distance from the source point (represented by the crosshair) to the Rubber Stamp cursor remains fixed. This means that you can release the mouse, move the cursor, then continue to use the Rubber Stamp tool. The relative position of the source point and the Rubber Stamp cursor remain constant, but you will now be cloning pixels from a different part of the image.

Clone – Non-aligned

With the Aligned option off, the source point – where you first click – remains the same. If you stop dragging with the Rubber Stamp cursor, move to a different part of the image, then start dragging again, the pixels you clone continue to come from the original source point.

The Pattern Stamp Tool

The Pattern Stamp tool works in a similar way to the Rubber Stamp tool, but it paints with a predefined area of pixels – the pattern – rather than from a variable source point in the image.

1   To define a pattern, select an area to use as a pattern (using the rectangular marquee tool: ⬚ – see page 98), then choose Edit > Define Pattern.

2   Choose the Pattern Stamp Tool. Check your brush size, position your cursor on the image, then click and drag to paint with the pattern.

Pattern – Aligned

With the Aligned option selected, even if you stop dragging and then restart, the pattern aligns seamlessly.

Pattern – Non-aligned

This option paints with the predefined pattern, but does not align seamlessly if you stop dragging and then restart dragging.

Use All Layers

Select this option if you want to sample pixels from all layers when you define a source point. Leave this option deselected to sample pixels from the target layer only.

The Dodge, Burn and Sponge Tools (O)

The Dodge, Burn, Saturate/Desaturate group of tools are collectively called the 'Toning' tools. The Dodge and Burn tools are based on the traditional photographic technique of decreasing the amount of exposure given to a specific area on a print to lighten it (dodging), or increasing the exposure to darken areas (burning-in).

The Dodge Tool
Use the Dodge tool to lighten pixels in your image.

You cannot use the Dodge, Burn or Saturate/ Desaturate tools on an image in Bitmap or Indexed Colour mode.

1 To lighten areas of an image, select the Dodge tool. Remember to choose an appropriate brush size. A soft-edged brush usually creates the smoothest result. If the Toning Tools Options palette is not showing, you can double-click the Dodge tool to show it.

2 Set the Midtone/Shadow/Highlight pop-up to limit changes to the middle range of greys, the dark or light areas of the image respectively, and also set Exposure to control the intensity of the tool.

It's a good idea to use a low exposure setting when you lighten areas of an image and build up the effect gradually.

3 Position your cursor on the image, then click and drag to lighten the pixels. Release the mouse then drag across the pixels again to intensify the effect.

The Burn Tool

Use the Burn tool to darken pixels in your image.

1 To darken areas of an image, select the Burn tool. Remember to choose an appropriate brush size. A soft-edged brush usually creates the smoothest result. If the Burn Options palette is not showing, you can double-click the Burn tool to show it.

2 Set the Midtone/Shadow/Highlight pop-up to limit changes to the middle range of greys, the dark or light areas of the image respectively, and also set Exposure.

3 Position your cursor on the image, then click and drag to lighten the pixels. Release the mouse then drag across the pixels again to intensify the effect.

In Greyscale Mode, the Sponge tool has the effect of increasing or decreasing contrast.

The Sponge Tool

You can use the Sponge tool when you want to subtly increase or decrease colour saturation in areas of your image.

1 To saturate/desaturate areas of an image, select the Sponge tool. Remember to select an appropriate brush size. If the Sponge Options palette is not showing, you can double-click the Sponge tool.

Each Toning tool retains its own settings when you switch to the other tools in the same group.

2 Set options for Saturate/ Desaturate and Pressure.

3 Position your cursor on the image, then click and drag to alter the saturation.

The Eraser Tool (E)

Use the Eraser tool to erase portions of your image. The Eraser rubs out to the background colour when you are working on the Background layer. It erases to transparency when you are working on any other layer, provided that the Preserve Transparency option is off.

Use the Brushes palette to specify the Eraser size when using the tool in Paintbrush, Pencil and Airbrush mode.

1 To erase areas of your image, double-click the Eraser tool to show the Eraser Options palette. Use the palette to specify Type, Opacity, Fade, Wet Edges and Erase to History options.

2 Click and drag on your image to erase to the background colour or transparency, depending on the layer on which you are working.

Hold down alt/ Alt with the Eraser tool selected to access the Erase to History option temporarily. Click and drag across modified areas of the image to restore them to the specified state in the History palette.

Opacity
Use the opacity setting to create the effect of partially erasing pixels.

Mode
Use the Erasing Mode pop-up to choose an erase mode. The default is Paintbrush.

Erase to History
Use the Erase to History option to return pixels to their status at a particular state in the History palette. Click in the History Brush column in the History palette to set the state to which the Erase to History option returns pixels.

The Magic Eraser (E)

Use the Magic Eraser tool to erase pixels on a layer to transparency. The Magic Eraser works best when you want to remove the background pixels around a hard-edged object.

The Magic Eraser tool erases pixels based on a tolerance level, similar to the way in which the Magic Wand works. (See page 105 for information on the Magic Wand.)

The Magic Eraser tool is grouped with the Eraser tool. Press and hold on the Eraser tool to access the tools in the tool group. You can also use the keyboard shortcut, Shift+E to cycle through the Eraser tools.

1 To use the Magic Eraser tool, first select the layer on which you want to work.

2 Double-click the Magic Eraser tool to show the Magic Eraser Options palette if it is not already showing.

3 Enter a tolerance value. Set a low tolerance value to erase only those pixels that are very similar in colour value to the pixel on which you first click. Set a high tolerance value to select a wider range of pixels.

The Tolerance value extends or limits the number of pixels that are erased.

Magic Eraser Options	▶
Tolerance: 32	Opacity: 100 ▶ %
☐ Use All Layers	☑ Anti-aliased
	☑ Contiguous

4 Set an Opacity value of 100% to erase pixels completely. Set a lower Opacity value to create a partially transparent effect.

If you use the Magic Eraser on the Background Layer, Photoshop automatically converts the layer to Layer O.

5 Select the Use All Layers option to erase pixels based on a sample that takes into account colour values from all visible layers, not only the currently active layer.

6 Select the Anti-aliased option to create a smoother edge when pixels are erased. (See page 84 for further information on anti-aliasing).

7 Select the Contiguous option to erase only pixels that fall within the tolerance value specified, and that are adjacent to each other. This option erases continuous areas of pixels. Deselect the Contiguous option if you want the Magic Eraser to erase all pixels that fall within the tolerance value anywhere in the image.

8 Position the cursor, then click to erase pixels that fall within the tolerance value.

The Background Eraser (E)

Use the Background Eraser tool when you are working on a layer to erase pixels to transparency. You can set tolerance and sampling values to control the level of transparency and the sharpness of its boundary edges.

The Background Eraser cursor displays a crosshair at the centre of the brush cursor. This indicates the tool's 'hotspot' – the point at which the tool's settings have greatest effect.

1 To erase pixels on a layer, select the Background Eraser tool. Select a layer on which you want to work.

The settings you choose have greatest effect at the hotspot. The strength of the effect diminishes further away from the hotspot.

2 Double-click the Background Eraser tool to show it's Options palette.

3 Choose Contiguous to remove adjacent pixels that fall within the tolerance setting. (Discontiguous erases pixels throughout the image, Find Edges preserves sharp edges along objects).

4 Set a Tolerance value (using the tolerance field), or drag the Tolerance slider. Set a low tolerance value to limit the effect to pixels that are very similar in colour value to pixels at the 'hotspot'. Set a high tolerance value to erase a broader range of similar colours.

5 Choose a Sampling option. Select Continuous to erase all colours that you drag the Background Eraser tool across. Select Once to erase pixels that are the same colour as the pixel on which you first click. This is useful when you want to erase areas of solid colour. Select Background Swatch only if you want to erase areas containing the currently set Background colour.

6 Select the Protect Foreground Colour if you want to prevent the tool from any pixels that match the currently set Foreground colour.

Be careful about the hotspot – keep it away from pixels in the layer that you don't want to erase. Modify your settings if you find that you are erasing pixels you don't want to erase.

7 Choose a Brush size from the Brushes palette.

8 Position our cursor on a layer, then drag to erase pixels on the layer to transparency, based on the settings you have chosen.

Making Selections

One of the most important techniques when using Photoshop is making selections. When you make a selection, you are selecting an area of the image to which you want to make changes, and isolating the remainder of the image so that it is not affected by changes. A selection is indicated on-screen by a selection marquee – sometimes referred to as the 'marching ants' border.

Covers

The Marquee Selection Tool (M) | 98

Marquee Options | 99

Moving Selections | 100

The Lasso Tools (L) | 102

The Magic Wand Tool (W) | 105

Feathering Selections | 106

Modifying Selections | 108

The Grow and Similar Commands | 109

Pasting Into Selections | 110

The Defringe Command | 111

Filling a Selection | 112

Copying and Pasting Selections | 113

Transforming Selections | 114

Chapter Eight

The Marquee Selection Tool (M)

The Marquee selection tools allow you to drag with the mouse to make selections. You can make rectangular or elliptical selections by choosing the appropriate tool.

1 To make a rectangular or oval selection, choose the Rectangular or Elliptical Marquee tool.

2 Position your cursor on the image, then click and drag to define the area you want to select. When you release the cursor you will see a dotted rectangular or oval marquee defining the area of the selection.

3 You can reposition the selection marquee if you need to. Make sure the Marquee tool is still selected, position your cursor inside the selection marquee (the cursor changes shape), then click and drag. You can move selection marquees with any of the Selection tools.

4 With the Marquee tool selected, you can deselect a selection by clicking inside or outside the selection marquee. Alternatively, you can choose Select > Deselect.

Marquee Options

You can use the Marquee Options palette to make changes to the way in which the Marquee tools work.

You can only have one selection active at a time, although a selection can consist of several non-contiguous areas.

1 Double-click the Marquee tool. The Marquee Options palette will appear if it is not already showing. Alternatively, select a Marquee tool, then choose Window > Show Options.

2 Use the Style pop-up to create settings for making proportional selections, or selections of a fixed size.

The Anti-aliased option is available in the Elliptical Marquee, Lasso and Magic Wand Options palettes.

3 The Anti-aliased option is an important control when using bitmap applications such as Photoshop. Select anti-aliased to create a slightly blurred, soft edge around the selection and the pixels that surround the selection. Using Anti-aliased helps avoid creating unwanted jagged edges.

Choose Select > Reselect to reselect your most recent selection. You can use the Reselect command even if you have performed operations and commands on the image since you deselected.

4 Use the Feather entry field to create a soft, feathered edge. (See pages 106–107 in this chapter.)

Moving Selections

You can use the Selection tools to reposition a selection border, but you must use the Move tool if you want to move pixels from one location to another.

| Make a selection. Select the Move tool and then position your cursor inside the Marquee selection border. Click and drag to move the selection. Alternatively, with the Marquee, Lasso or Magic Wand tool still selected, hold down Command/Ctrl. The cursor changes temporarily to the Move tool cursor. Click and drag to move the selected pixels.

When you move pixels on the Background layer, the area from which the pixels are moved is filled with the current background colour.

As long as the selection border remains selected, you can continue to move the pixels. Whilst the selection is active, the pixels in the selection 'float' above the underlying pixels, without replacing them.

2 To 'defloat' the pixels so that they replace the underlying pixels, choose Select > Deselect if you have the Move tool selected. If you used Command/Ctrl with a Marquee or Lasso tool selected, click outside the selection marquee. If you used Command/Ctrl with the Magic Wand tool selected, choose Select > Deselect. As soon as you deselect, the pixels on the Background layer that were underneath the floating selection – the underlying pixels – are now completely replaced by the pixels in the floating selection.

3 Notice that the area that the pixels in the selection were moved from is filled with the currently selected background colour. (In a bitmap image, you cannot have an area where there are no pixels.)

4 To move a selection and make a copy of it at the same time, hold down alt/Alt before you drag with the Move tool. Alternatively, with a selection tool selected, hold down Command/Ctrl+alt/Alt,

then click and drag. The cursor turns into a double-headed arrow, indicating that you are copying the selection.

5 You can turn a 'floating' selection into a layer by choosing Layer > New > Layer Via Cut. (See Chapter 9 – Layers for further information.)

The Lasso Tools (L)

You can use the Lasso tool to make freeform selections by clicking and dragging. It is a useful tool for selecting irregular areas and for quickly adding to or subtracting from selections made with the Magic Wand tool.

Hold down Shift, then click and drag around an area to add it to the selection. Hold down alt/Alt, then click and drag around an area to remove it from the selection.

| Double-click the Lasso tool to show the Lasso Options palette if it is not already showing. Set Feather and Anti-aliased options.

2 Position your cursor on the image. The cursor changes to the Lasso cursor. Click and drag around the part of the image you want to select. Make sure your cursor comes back to the start point. If you release before reaching the start point, Photoshop completes the selection with a straight line. A dotted marquee defines the selected area.

Polygon Lasso

If you have a feather amount set in the Lasso Options palette, you will not end up with sharp corners on the selection.

Use the Polygon Lasso tool to create a freeform selection with straight line segments.

| Select the Polygon Lasso tool. Position your cursor on the image, then click; move the cursor, then click... and so on, until you have defined the area you want to select.

2 Click back at the start point to complete the selection. A small circle appears at the bottom right of the cursor to indicate the start. Alternatively, you can double-click to close the selection marquee.

The Magnetic Lasso

The Magnetic Lasso Tool is most useful when you want to select an object or an area of the image which contrasts strongly with the area surrounding it.

1 Press and hold on the Lasso tool, to select the Magnetic Lasso tool from the tool group. Click on the edge of the object you want to select to place the first fastening point.

2 Either, move the cursor along the edge of the object, or click and drag along the edge to draw a freehand segment. As you move along the edge of the object, the 'active' segment of the selection border snaps to the most clearly defined edge in the image (in the close proximity of the cursor). Fastening points are added automatically, at intervals, as you drag.

A fastening point anchors the Selection Border in place as you create the selection. Fastening Points disappear when you close the selection border. The Magnetic Lasso adds fastening points at intervals to the selection border to anchor the segments.

3 Click on the edge of the shape if you need to add a fastening point manually. Continue moving the cursor, or dragging and clicking, to continue making the selection border.

4 To close the selection border, position your cursor on the start point, (a small circle at the cursor indicates that you are on the start point) then click. Alternatively, double-click; or press the Enter/Return key. Photoshop will create a segment from the point you have reached to the start point of the selection border. To close the selection border with a straight line segment, hold down alt/ALT and double-click.

Magnetic Lasso Options

As with all the tools you use in Photoshop, after you have clicked on the tool to select it, but before you start to use it, check the setting for the tool in the appropriate tool options palette.

Double-click the Magnetic Lasso tool to show the Magnetic Lasso Options palette if it is not already showing. (Or use Window > Show Options.)

Lasso Width

Enter a value between 1–40 to specify a detection width. The Magnetic Lasso tool detects edges only within the specified distance from the pointer.

Frequency

this setting determines the rate at which Fastening points are set. Enter a value between 0–100. The higher the value you set, the more frequently fastening points are placed.

Edge Contrast

If the object you are trying to select has high contrast (ie, well defined edges) use higher Lasso Width and Edge Contrast settings. For objects with less well defined edges, use lower Lasso Width and Edge Contrast settings.

Enter a value between 1–100%. This value determines how sensitive the Magnetic Lasso tool is to edges in the image. Higher values select edges that contrast strongly with their background. Lower values select edges that have smaller amounts of contrast.

The Magic Wand Tool (W)

The Magic Wand tool selects continuous areas of colour in an image, based on a tolerance setting. Low tolerance settings create a very limited selection of colour. Higher settings select a wider range of pixels. The tool is good for selecting consistently coloured areas.

To add to a selection using the Magic Wand tool, hold down Shift, then click on an unselected part of the image.

1 Before creating a selection using the Magic Wand tool, check the tolerance setting. Double-click the Magic Wand tool to display the Magic Wand Options palette,

or choose Window > Show Options to show the Options palette, then select the Magic Wand tool. Enter a tolerance value from 0–255. If you set a tolerance value of 255, you will select every pixel in the image.

Typically, you will fine-tune Magic Wand selections using a combination of the other selection tools, together with the Grow and Similar commands.

2 Click on the image to select pixels of similar colour value. All adjacent pixels that are within the tolerance range are selected. Adjust the default setting of 32 as necessary to make the selection you require.

3 Deselect the Contiguous option to select pixels throughout the image that fall within the Tolerance setting. The result is similar to using the Similar command (see page 109).

You cannot use the Magic Wand tool in Bitmap mode.

4 To deselect a selection marquee when the Magic Wand tool is selected, click inside the selection marquee. If you click outside the selection marquee, you will create another selection based around the pixel where you clicked.

Feathering Selections

You can define a feathered edge when you make selections using the Lasso tools and the Marquee tools.

You can use the Feather option to control the degree to which the edge of a selection is softened or faded. Feathering a selection creates a transition boundary between the selection and the surrounding pixels, which can cause a loss of detail.

| Double-click one of the Lasso or the Marquee selection tools. The Options palette for the tool appears if it was not already showing.

Check the Options palette before you make a selection to make sure that there isn't a feather amount set if you don't want one.

2 In the Options palette, set a feather value, e.g. 10. You can set a value from 1 to 250 pixels. The amount you set depends on the effect you want to achieve.

3 Create a selection using either the Marquee or Lasso tool. When you move the selection you will see the feathered edge around the selection and also where you move the selection from.

When you set a feather amount, the selection you make may appear more 'rounded' than you expect. This is caused by the feather value.

4 Alternatively, you can make a selection and then choose Select > Feather. Enter a value for the Feather radius.

Creating a Vignette

You can use the feathering option to create a vignette effect – a soft, fading edge to an image.

1 Before you begin, make sure your background colour is set to white (see Chapter Five – Defining Colours). Then set a feather value in the Options palette for the selection tool you are using.

2 Next, create a selection, which can be a regular or irregular shape.

3 Choose Select > Inverse. This reverses the selection – selecting all the pixels that were previously not selected.

Feathering, unlike anti-aliasing, blurs the inside and outside of a selection boundary.

4 Press Delete (Mac) or Backspace (Windows) to delete the area surrounding your selection, leaving a feathered edge.

Modifying Selections

There are many instances when you need to add to or subtract from a selection. You can use any combination of selection tools to make the selection you want. For example, you might start by making a selection with the Magic Wand tool, then add to the selection using the Lasso tool.

HOT TIP

For complex selections, it can be quite useful to hide the dotted selection border temporarily, in order to see the selected pixels more clearly. Choose View > Hide Edges to hide the selection border. The selection remains active; you have simply hidden the border. Choose View > Show Edges to redisplay the selection border.

1 To add to an existing selection, hold down the Shift key, then click and drag to create another selection marquee that intersects the existing selection marquee.

2 You can use the same technique to create non-adjoining selections. Although the selections may be in different parts of the image, they count and act as one selection. So, for example, if you apply a filter, the effect will be apparent in all the selection marquees.

3 Hold down Shift and use the Lasso tool to quickly loop around small areas that the Magic Wand tool typically misses out from its selection.

4 To subtract from a selection, hold down alt/Alt, then click and drag with a selection tool to intersect the existing selection marquee. The area defined by the intersecting marquee will be removed from the original selection.

The Grow and Similar Commands

The Grow and Similar commands are very useful when used in conjunction with the Magic Wand tool to add to a selection. Both work according to the tolerance setting set in the Magic Wand Options palette.

The Grow command selects contiguous or adjoining areas of colour based on the tolerance setting in the Magic Wand Options palette.

1 Make a selection. Check that the Tolerance setting in the Magic Wand Options palette is appropriate.

2 Choose Select > Grow. Pixels which fall within the Tolerance setting and are adjacent to pixels already in the selection are added to the selection.

The Similar command selects non-adjacent pixels that fall within the same tolerance setting as set in the Magic Wand Options palette.

1 Make a selection using any of the selection tools. Check that the Tolerance setting in the Magic Wand Options palette is appropriate.

2 Choose Select > Similar. Pixels throughout the image that fall within the Tolerance setting are selected.

Pasting Into Selections

Pasting into selections is a useful technique for compositing images.

When you paste into a selection, the selection from the clipboard will be rendered at the resolution of the destination document. This means that the selection from the source document will change size if the resolution of the two documents is different.

1 Create a selection in the destination window.

2 Open the source document, then make the selection you want to paste into the destination document. Choose Edit > Copy to copy the selection to the clipboard.

3 Click in the destination image window. The selection should still be active. Choose Edit > Paste Into to paste the clipboard selection into the selected area.

Make sure the layer mask is selected, then paint with black to add to the mask, or paint with white to subtract from the mask. (See pages 164–165, 'Layer Masks'.)

4 Use the Move tool to reposition the pasted selection relative to the original selection.

5 The Paste Into command has created a layer mask. The layer is active, indicated by the paintbrush icon in the Layers palette, which means that you can edit the layer. To edit the mask, click the mask icon in the Layers palette. A small circle replaces the paintbrush, indicating that the layer mask is selected.

The Defringe Command

You can drag a selection from one window to another image window. This is useful when creating a composite image. Defringe is useful when you use this technique, as it helps to blend the selection into its new environment.

1 To drag a selection from one image window to another, first make a selection in the source window. Select the Move tool, position the Move cursor inside the selection, then click and drag into the destination window.

2 When you release the mouse button, the selection appears in the destination window on a new layer. The destination window becomes the active window, and the new layer is the active layer. Check to see if there are unwanted pixels causing a halo effect around the edge of the selection.

A width setting of 1 or 2 pixels is usually sufficient to defringe a pasted or moved selection.

3 To defringe the moved selection, make sure the newly created layer is active, and make sure Preserve Transparency is deselected. Choose Layer > Matting > Defringe. Enter a value for the width, then OK the dialogue box. The selection should now blend in better.

Filling a Selection

You can use the Fill dialogue box to fill an entire layer or a selection.

1   To fill a selection, first define either a foreground or background colour that you want to fill with, then make a selection. Choose Edit > Fill. Use the Contents pop-up to choose the fill type. You can also set Opacity for the fill and a Blending Mode. OK the dialogue box.

See pages 82–83 for a description of the blending modes.

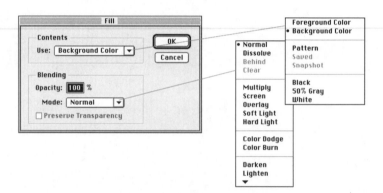

2   To fill a selection with a pattern, first define the pattern by making a selection, then choosing Edit > Define Pattern.

3   Choose Edit > Fill. Choose Pattern from the Contents pop-up. OK the dialogue box to fill the selection with the pattern.

Copying and Pasting Selections

You can use the clipboard to copy and past selections within the same image and into other images.

A useful technique for selecting a simple image, like the runner on this page, is the Inverse selection command. Use the Magic Wand tool to select the background, then choose Select > Inverse to reverse the selection. The areas that represent the runner are now selected.

1 To copy a selection, first make a selection using any of the selection tools. Choose Edit > Copy.

2 To paste the selection into the same image, choose Edit > Paste. The selection is pasted into the image on its own layer. (For information on working with layers, see Chapter Nine, 'Layers'.)

3 To paste the selection into another image, click on the other image window if it is already open, or use File > Open to open another image. Choose Edit > Paste to paste the selection from the clipboard onto a new layer in the active image.

4 You can also drag a selection from one image window into another. You need two images open – the source and the destination windows. Make a selection in the source window, select the Move tool, position your cursor within the selection, then click and drag into the destination window. The selection appears on its own layer.

Use the Defringe command (see page 111) to help a pasted or dragged selection blend into its new surroundings.

Transforming Selections

The ability to transform a selection's bounding box enables you to fine tune selections, distort selections and make selections that were previously difficult to achieve.

The Transform Selection bounding box transforms the selection border only. It does not transform the pixels within the selection.

1 To transform a selection, choose Select > Transform Selection. A bounding box with eight handles appears around the selection. A Point of Origin marker appears at the centre of the bounding box.

2 To scale a selection, click and drag a handle. The cursor becomes a bi-directional arrow (). To scale a selection in proportion, hold down Shift then drag a handle.

Drag the point of origin to a new location to specify the point around which transformations take place.

3 To rotate a selection, position your cursor just outside the selection border. The cursor changes to a bi-directional, curved arrow (↱↲). Click and drag in a circular direction.

4 To distort the selection boundary, hold down Command/Ctrl then drag a corner handle.

5 To create a perspective effect on the selection border, hold down Command/Ctrl+alt/ Alt+Shift, then drag a corner handle.

6 To shear a selection border, hold down Command/Ctrl, then click and drag a centre top/bottom or centre left/right handle.

7 Press the Esc key to remove the transform bounding box without applying any of the changes. Press return/Enter, or double-click inside the bounding box to accept the transformation.

Layers

Layers introduce a considerable degree of flexibility into the way in which you can work in Photoshop. Layers allow you to keep various elements of your image separate so that you can make changes without deleting or changing the underlying pixels in the image.

Each additional layer you create increases the file size of the image. When you have finished editing your image, you can selectively merge layers into each other. You will need to do this to use your image in QuarkXPress or Adobe PageMaker. You should note that you can only save images with layers in Photoshop format.

Covers

Working with Layers | 116

Merging and Flattening Layers | 118

Moving Layers Between Images | 119

Linking Layers | 120

Adjustment Layers | 121

Transparency | 123

New Layer Commands | 124

Layer Effects | 125

Managing Layer Effects | 127

Transforming Layers | 129

The Extract Command | 131

Fine Tuning Extractions | 134

Chapter Nine

Working with Layers

When you create or open an image for the first time, it consists of one default layer called Background.

To access the Layers palette, choose Window > Show Layers.

1   To create a new layer, either click once on the New Layer icon at the bottom of the Layers palette, or use the pop-up menu in the Layers palette and choose New Layer.

New layers are auto-matically created when you use the Type tool to add text to an image, when you drag or copy a selection into an image, and also when you drag a layer from one document into another.

2   Enter a name for the layer in the New Layer dialogue box. You can also choose Opacity and Blending Mode settings at this stage if you want to.

3   OK the dialogue box, or press Return/Enter. The new layer appears in the Layers palette above the previously highlighted layer. Notice also that the file size in the Document Sizes status bar area increases when you paint on the layer or add pixels to the layer.

To edit Layer Options for a Layer, double-click the layer name. The Layer Options dialogue box appears. Make changes as necessary, then OK the dialogue box.

4   To delete a layer, click on the layer to select it. Then choose Delete Layer from the pop-up menu in the Layers palette. Click Yes or No in the Delete Layer warning box. Alternatively, drag the Layer name onto the Wastebasket icon at the bottom of the Layers palette.

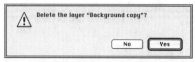

Selecting, Hiding and Showing Layers

You can only work on one layer at a time. This is often referred to as the 'target' or active layer.

1 Click on the layer name in the Layers palette to make it active. The layer name will highlight and the paintbrush icon will appear in the second column on the left of the palette.

You can nudge the contents of a selected layer in 1-pixel increments by pressing the arrow keys when the Move tool is selected.

2 To hide a layer, click on the eye icon in the leftmost column of the Layers palette. To show a layer, click in the leftmost column to bring back the eye icon.

Reordering Layers

It is often necessary to reorder the stacking position of layers, in order to control which layers appear in front of other layers.

You can move pixels in a layer beyond the edge of your picture. These non-visible pixels will be saved with the document. These non-visible pixels are lost when you flatten the image.

1 To change the layering order, click and drag the layer name you want to reposition. Notice the black horizontal bar that appears as you move the layer upwards or downwards. Release the mouse when the black bar appears in the position to which you want the layer moved.

Repositioning Layers

You can reposition the entire contents of a layer using the Move tool.

1 Click on the layer you want to move in the Layers palette. Select the Move tool, then position your cursor anywhere on the image. Click and drag to move the layer.

Merging and Flattening Layers

Use the Merge commands to combine two or more layers into one layer. This is useful for keeping file size down and for consolidating elements on different layers into a single manageable layer or unit.

1. To merge all the visible layers in your document, first hide any layers you don't want to merge, make sure one of the layers you want to merge is active, then choose Merge Visible from the pop-up menu in the Layers palette, or choose Layer > Merge Visible.

2. To merge a layer with the layer below it, first select the layer, then choose Merge Down from the pop-up menu, or choose Layer > Merge Down.

Flattening Images

When you flatten an image, you end up with a Background layer only. This reduces the file size. Flatten an image when you have finished creating and positioning the elements of your composite image, and are ready to save the file in a suitable format for placing in a page layout application.

To flatten an image, make sure that all the layers you want to keep are visible. Choose Flatten Image from the Layers palette pop-up menu, or choose Layers > Flatten Image.

Moving Layers Between Images

The layer you move into the destination image window is rendered at the resolution of the destination window. This may cause the elements on the moved layer to appear larger or smaller than in the original window. To avoid surprises, make sure that the source and destination images are at the same resolution.

Also, if the modes of the two images are different, the layer you move will be converted to match the mode of the destination window.

You can copy a complete layer from one Photoshop document to another, similar to the way you move a selection from one document to another.

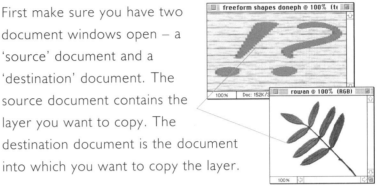

1   First make sure you have two document windows open – a 'source' document and a 'destination' document. The source document contains the layer you want to copy. The destination document is the document into which you want to copy the layer.

2   Click in the source document window to make it active. Position your cursor on the layer in the Layers palette, then drag the layer you want to copy from the source document into the destination document window. You will see a bounding box indicating the layer you are copying.

Use the Defringe command (see page 111) to remove any fringe around pixels on a layer that you copy from one image to another.

3   Position the layer and then release the mouse. The layer is positioned above the previously active layer in the Layers palette of the destination document. The destination document is now the active image window.

Linking Layers

Linking layers is useful when you want to keep elements of an image on separate layers, but you need to move the layers maintaining the exact positional relationship of each.

1. To move the foreground object with its shadow (which is on a separate layer), show the Layers palette (Window > Show Layers) and make sure that one of the layers you want to link is active.

The principle of linking layers works, even if the layers are not next to each other in the Layers palette.

2. Click in the empty box to the right of the eye icon of the layer you want to link. A chain icon appears in the box, indicating that the layer is linked. When you make the linked layer active, the chain and paintbrush icons switch to indicate the layer you are working on.

3. Use the Move tool to reposition the elements on the linked layers as one.

4. You can link multiple layers using the same technique.

5. To unlink a layer, click the chain icon. The layer is now completely independent again.

Adjustment Layers

Using an adjustment layer is like positioning a lens above the pixels on the layers below it to change their appearance. If you don't like the result, you can edit the adjustment layer to achieve the result you want, or you can discard the adjustment layer. When you are satisfied with the result you can implement the adjustment layer as a permanent change.

An adjustment layer is created above the currently active layer. Its settings are applied to the layers below it and do not affect layers above.

1 Select a layer in the Layers palette. The adjustment layer will be positioned above the currently active layer. From the Layers palette pop-up choose New Adjustment Layer, or choose Layer > New > Adjustment.

You can restack adjustment layers as any other layer.

2 Choose a type from the Type pop-up menu. This automatically becomes the name for the layer. Enter a different name if desired. Set Opacity and Blending Mode at this stage if you want to. Click OK.

3 Depending on the type of adjustment layer you chose, the appropriate dialogue box opens. Create the settings you want to experiment with. OK the dialogue box.

4 The new adjustment layer appears in the Layers palette as the active layer. The settings you created are now applied to all layers below the adjustment layer.

5 Click the eye icon to hide/show the preview of the changes brought about by the adjustment layer settings. Double-click the adjustment layer to re-enter the appropriate adjustment dialogue box to make changes to the settings.

The adjustment layer settings do not have a permanent effect on pixels until the layer is merged with other layers, or the image is flattened.

6 Drag the adjustment layer into the wastebasket if you want to discard the settings.

7 When you are ready to make the settings of the adjustment layer permanent, either use one of the Merge commands from the pop-up, or flatten the image.

Transparency

Layers have transparent areas where there are no pixels on the layer, allowing you to see through to pixels on other layers. Preserve Transparency enables you to control which pixels are affected when you paint on or edit a layer.

Hold down alt/ Alt and click an eye icon to hide all layers other than the one you click on. Hold down alt/ Alt and click the same eye icon again to show all layers.

1   To see transparent areas of a layer, hide all other layers by clicking on their eye icons. The transparent areas of the layer are represented by the checkerboard.

2   To work on a layer without affecting any of the transparent areas, select a layer, then make sure you select the Preserve Transparency option. In this example, painting with the Airbrush tool colours only existing pixels and does not affect the transparent areas of the layer where there are no pixels.

Transparent areas on a layer are indicated by the checkerboard pattern.

3   To colour existing pixels as well as the currently transparent areas of a layer, click the Preserve Transparency option to switch it off. Now when you paint on the layer or edit it in other ways, the transparent areas can be coloured – they are no longer protected from changes you make.

To select all pixels on a layer, hold down Command/Ctrl and click on the layer name in the Layers palette.

4   You can make pixels on individual layers semi-transparent by changing the Opacity setting for the layer.

New Layer Commands

The New Layer Via Cut (Command/Ctrl+Shift+J) and the New Layer Via Copy (Command/Ctrl+J) commands are essential options when creating layers. Use these commands to either cut or copy selected pixels to a new layer.

1 Start by making a selection. Then chose Layer > New > Layer Via Copy to create a new layer containing a copy of the selected pixels. The new layer is automatically named Layer 1, etc, depending on the number of layers already in the document.

Layer...	⇧⌘N
Adjustment Layer...	
Background	
Layer Via Copy	⌘J
Layer Via Cut	⇧⌘J

To move pixels on a layer, first make sure the layer is active, select the Move tool, position your cursor in the image window, then click and drag to move the pixels on the layer.

2 Make a selection, then choose New Layer Via Cut to cut the selected pixels to a new layer. Notice when you reposition the pixels on the new layer, the area on the Background layer from which they were cut is filled with the current background colour.

Layer Effects

Using the Layer Effects sub-menu, you can now create sophisticated layer effects such as soft shadows, bevelled and embossed edges, and inner and outer glows quickly and easily.

This example consists of 3 layers – a White background layer, a coloured circle on its own layer and a coloured triangle on another layer.

The following example uses Bevel and Emboss options to demonstrate the principles of using layer effects.

You can apply multiple Layer Effects to the same layer.

1 To apply a Layer Effect, click on a layer in the Layers palette to make it active. Choose Layer > Effects > Bevel & Emboss.

2 Use the Effect pop-up if you want to apply a different effect. Make sure the Apply option is selected and click the Preview option to see the effect applied in the image window with the default settings.

3 Adjust settings for the Highlight and Shadow edges of the effect. It is a good idea initially to leave the Modes set to Screen and Multiply respectively. Experiment with the Opacity sliders to create a more subtle effect.

4 Use the Style pop-up to choose a particular bevel or emboss type.

5 Enter a value in the Angle entry box to control the direction of the light source. Press and hold the black pop-up triangle to access the Angle disc if you prefer.

6 Use the Depth entry box or slider to adjust the height of the effect. Use the Blur entry box or slider to control the spread of the effect.

7 Select the Up/Down radio button to light the effect from above or below. OK the dialogue box when you are satisfied with the settings.

8 Notice in the Layers palette an 'f' symbol (𝑓) on the layer, indicating that there is a layer effect applied to the layer. Whilst the 'f' symbol appears the layer effect remains editable.

Settings for
the circle
layer

Managing Layer Effects

Once you have created a layer effect you can continue to edit the effect and you can use a variety of commands from the Layer Effects sub-menu to manage the effects.

1   To edit the settings used to create a layer effect, make sure the appropriate layer is active, then use Layer > Effects to return to the layer effect you want to edit. Make changes to the settings, then OK the dialogue box. You can continue to adjust settings as long as the layer displays the layer effects icon.

Once you merge a layer with a layer effect applied to it, you can no longer adjust the layer effect settings.

2   To temporarily disable layer effects on all layers, not just the active layer, choose Layer > Effects > Hide All Effects. Repeat the process to show all layer effects.

3   To keep the angle of the light source constant if you are using multiple layer effects, choose Layer > Effects > Set Global Angle. Enter a value for the Angle in the Global Angle entry box. OK the dialogue box. Make sure you select the Use Global option when you create multiple layer effects in the Effects dialogue box.

4   To copy exact layer effect settings from one layer to another, first select a layer with a layer effect applied to it, then choose Copy Effects from the Effects sub-menu. Click on another layer in the Layers palette. Choose Paste Effects from the Effects sub-menu.

5 To permanently remove layer effects from a layer, make sure you select the appropriate layer, then choose Layer > Effects > Clear Effects.

6 Layer Effects automate procedures that in the past you had to perform yourself. Use the Create Layer command from the Effects sub-menu to separate the layer effect into the multiple layers that Photoshop has used to create the effect. This can be useful if you need to edit specific parts of the effect.

Transforming Layers

You cannot transform the Background layer in an image.

Once you have moved pixels to a new layer you can then transform the layer. Using Free Transform you can scale, rotate, distort, skew and create perspective effects.

1 Make sure the layer is active. Choose Edit > Free Transform. A bounding box with handles appears around the pixels on the layer.

2 To scale a layer, drag a handle on the bounding box. To scale in proportion, hold down Shift, then drag a corner handle.

To use Perspective and Distort transformations on a type layer, you must first render (convert to pixels) the type layer – Layer > Type > Render Layer.

3 To rotate a layer, position your cursor slightly outside the bounding box. The cursor changes to a bi-directional arrow. Drag in a circular direction. You can drag the point of origin marker to a new position to specify the point around which the rotation takes place.

4 To skew the layer, hold down Command/Ctrl+Shift, then drag either the centre top/bottom, or the centre left/right handle.

The Transform sub-menu (Edit > Transform) gives alternative options for transforming layers.

5 To reposition the layer, position your cursor inside the bounding box, then click and drag.

6 To create perspective, hold down Command/Ctrl+alt/Alt+Shift, then drag a corner handle.

7 To distort the layer, hold down Command/Ctrl, then drag a corner handle. This allows you to move corner handles independently. Hold down Shift with the Command/Ctrl key to constrain the movement vertically or horizontally.

The advantage of Free Transform is that you can make multiple transformations, then either accept or discard the result.

8 To accept the transformation and remove the Transformation bounding box, press Return/Enter, or double-click inside the bounding box.

9 To revert to the original state without making changes, press the Esc key.

The Extract Command

Use the Extract command to isolate an object from its background; especially useful when the object has edges that are not clearly or distinctly defined, such as hair.

Make sure you are working on a layer to use the Extract command. If you perform the Extract command on the Background layer it becomes Layer 0 when you OK the dialogue box.

There are 4 steps to extracting an object from its background. First, highlight the edges of the object. Second, define the interior of the object. Third, preview the results of the extraction. Four, depending on the preview, fine tune the extraction, then OK the dialogue box.

1 To extract an object from its background, choose Image > Extract. Select the Edge Highlighter tool (B).

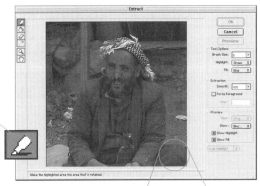

2 In the Tool Options area, set a brush size and choose a colour for the highlight edge from the Highlight pop-up.

Take your time, don't be tempted to rush the process of creating the highlighted edge.

Use the [or] keys to decrease/increase the brush size in single increments.

3 Zoom in on the image if necessary, then draw around the object you want to extract to define the edge. It is important to create a highlight that slightly overlaps both the edge of the foreground object and its background. Use a larger brush size to completely cover more delicate, intricate, 'wispy' areas of the foreground object, such as hair; use a smaller brush size to highlight sharper, more defined edges.

4 Use the Eraser tool to undo any mistakes you make with the Edge Highlighter tool. You cannot use the Undo command within the Extract dialogue box.

5 Make sure you completely enclose the object if it has a well-defined interior. It is not necessary to highlight edges where the object touches the edge of the image window.

6 Select the Fill tool (K). Click inside the highlight edge. The interior fills with the Fill colour set in the Tool Options area of the dialogue box.

7 Click the Preview button to preview the results. Use the Show pop-up in the Preview area to specify the background against which you see the extracted object. It can be helpful to preview against more than one background colour to pick up on any problem areas, before

Fine Tuning Extractions

After you preview the results of the extraction, you will need to fine tune it, before you OK the dialogue box.

1 To make adjustments to the extraction, select the Show Highlight option in the Preview area. The original highlight edge reappears.

2 Click the Show Fill option to show the original fill area for the extraction.

3 Choose Original from the View pop-up. The solid background against which you preview the results of the extraction disappears and the original background pixels reappear.

 Use the Smooth control in the Extraction area, if necessary, to improve the result of the extraction. The Smooth control can help remove stray artifacts from the extraction by feathering edges slightly.

4 Select the Fill tool, then click inside the Fill area. This removes the fill highlight. Use the Eraser tool to erase parts of the highlight edge and use the Edge Highlighter tool to redefine areas of the edge, as necessary.

5 When you have finished editing the highlight edge, select the Fill tool, then click inside the edge to recreate the fill area. Click the Preview button to preview your changes. Repeat the editing process as necessary until you are satisfied with the result, then click OK.

Working with Type

Use the Type tools in Adobe Photoshop when the type needs to be an essential ingredient of the image. Although Photoshop offers considerable flexibility and control over type, ultimately applications such as QuarkXPress and Adobe PageMaker provide better all round type handling capabilities if the type is not integral to the image itself. For example, if you are simply layering a headline across an image you will have greater flexibiltiy creating the text in a page layout application.

When you create type it automatically appears on its own layer. You can keep type editable until you are ready to render it as pixels. Once type is rendered as pixels you can use further Photoshop commands on it that are unavailable when the type exists as an editable type layer.

The Type Mask tools allow you to create complex selections in the shape of type characters.

You can choose different alignments vertically and horizontally for type, you can rotate it, fill it with a gradient, pattern or image, create translucent type and much more.

Covers

Creating Type | 136

Type Settings | 138

Editing and Selecting Type | 140

Vertical and Rotated Type | 142

Type Mask Tools | 143

Type and Layer Effects | 144

Chapter Ten

Creating Type

You can choose the Type tool, or the Vertical Type tool to enter type. Type is automatically placed onto a type layer which is saved with the document. Additional type layers add to the overall size of the file. You can work with type layers as you would with any other layer.

1 To enter type, select either the Type or the Vertical Type tool. Position your cursor on the image where you want the type to start. Click. This sets the text insertion point. The Type Tool dialogue box appears.

2 Create settings for Font and Style, Size and Leading.

3 Click the Colour Box to specify a colour for the type. This opens the Colour picker dialogue box. (See page 66 for information on using the Colour Picker dialogue box.)

Use the Move tool to reposition a layer, including editable type layers.

4 Select the Preview option if you want to see a preview of the type in the image window. (This option is not available when working in Multichannel, Bitmap or Indexed Colour modes.)

5 Select an alignment option. For horizontal type the options are left aligned, centred, right aligned. For Vertical type the options are align top, align vertical centre, align bottom.

When you create type in Multi-channel, Bitmap or Indexed Colour images, the type is placed directly onto the Background layer and it cannot be edited.

6 Click into the text entry window at the bottom of the dialogue box. Enter the text. The text appears formatted with the settings you have already created.

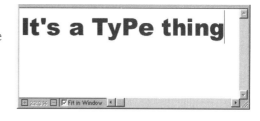

7 If you have selected the Preview option, you can drag the type preview in the image window to reposition the type.

8 Click OK or press Enter on the Numeric Keypad. The type is automatically placed on a new layer. The [T] icon indicates that this is a type layer and that the type layer is still editable.

Converting Type Layers

Convert a type layer to a standard layer when you no longer need to edit the text and its settings. The editable type is converted to pixels (rendered) which allows you the flexibility of using the full range of Photoshop commands and filters which are not available when type is on an editable type layer.

1 To convert type to a standard layer, click the type layer in the Layers palette.

2 Choose Layer > Type > Render Layer. The type layer becomes a standard layer and the [T] icon disappears to indicate this.

Type Settings

Font

Use the Font pop-up to choose from the list of fonts available on your system.

Size

Enter a value in the Size box for the size of your type. Use the Size pop-up to choose either points or pixels as the measurement system for type.

Leading

Leading controls the distance from one baseline of type to the next. Enter a leading value in the leading entry box. Leading is measured according to the size measurement option (points or pixels) that is selected. Photoshop applies a default leading value of 125% of the type size you have selected if you leave the leading box empty.

And the nights that have come between

Anti-Aliased

The anti-aliased option creates type with a slightly soft edge. It does this by blurring the pixels that form the edge of the type. Use this option to avoid unnecessary jagged edges in type, unless you are working with very small type.

Anti-aliased text has a softer edge, which is usually desirable, helping the type to blend into its background. Text that is not anti-aliased can look jagged. Choose an amount of anti-aliasing from the Anti-Alias pop-up.

Type, at very small sizes, can appear blurred if anti-aliasing is applied.

None
Crisp
Strong
✓ Smooth

None
Crisp
Strong
Smooth

Kerning and Tracking

In the Type Tool dialogue box you can create settings for Kerning and Tracking. Auto Kern is on by default. Deselect the Auto Kern option if you do not want the built-in pair kerning table for the font to be automatically applied.

In most instances, fractional character widths provides the best spacing for type. Switch off the Fractional Widths option when working with type below 20 points that is to be viewed on screen. If you leave the option selected, type characters may run together when displayed on a monitor screen.

1. To kern character pairs, click between the characters in the text entry window to place the text insertion bar. Deselect the Auto Kern option. You can now enter a value in the Kerning entry box. Negative characters move characters closer together. Positive values move characters apart.

2. For Tracking, highlight a range of text you want to track. Enter a value in the Tracking entry box.

Tracking = 84

Tracking = -36

Baseline Shift

The Baseline Shift control allows you to move highlighted characters above or below their original baseline to create a variety of effects.

1. To baseline shift characters, in the text entry window, make sure you highlight the characters you want to shift.

2. Enter a positive value to baseline shift upwards, enter a negative value to baseline shift downward.

Editing and Selecting Type

It is important to keep type layers editable until you are satisfied that you will not need to make further changes to any of the settings available in the Type Tool dialogue box. When you are satisfied with your type settings, you can convert the editable Type layer to a standard layer. You will then be able to use the full range of Photoshop commands and filters on the layer – but you will no longer be able to edit the text or its settings.

There are some transformations and commands that you can apply to an editable type layer without first having to convert it to a standard layer. For example, you can use the Transformation commands available in the Edit menu (with the exception of Perspective and Distort). You can also use all the Layer Effects in the Layer menu.

Editing Type Settings

1 To edit a type layer, make sure that the Layers palette is showing. Double-click the name of the type layer.

2 In the text entry area, highlight the text you want to change. Make changes to the setting in the Type Tool dialogue box. Click OK.

3 Click the [+] or [-] zoom buttons to change the magnification of the text as it appears in the text entry area. This does not affect the text as it will appear in your image. Alternatively, select the Fit in Window option to automatically scale the text to fit in the text entry area.

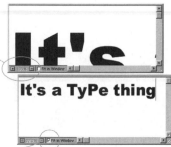

Selecting Text

Before you can make changes to settings for existing text, you must first select the range of text you want to change. You can now select either all the text on a type layer, or specific ranges of text in the text entry area of the Type Tool dialogue box to create mixed settings for type.

1 To select a specific range of text, click and drag across the text in the text entry area to highlight it.

2 Click in the text to place the text insertion point. This defines the start of the text you want to highlight. Move the cursor (do not press and drag), then hold down Shift and click to define the end of the range of text.

3 Double-click on a word to highlight one word.

4 Use Command/Ctrl+A to select all the text in the text entry area.

5 With the appropriate range of text highlighted you can then make changes to the settings. The changes you make apply to the highlighted text only.

Vertical and Rotated Type

Use the Vertical Type tool to create vertical type in the image. You can also create rotated vertical type.

1 To create vertical type, choose the Vertical Type tool. Click in the image window to specify the start position for the type. Create type settings as for standard type. Choose one of the Vertical Type Alignment options.

To change horizontal type into vertical type and vice versa, make sure the appropriate type layer is active, then choose Layer > Type > Vertical/ Horizontal.

2 To rotate vertical type, double-click the type layer to open the Type Tool dialogue box. Highlight the text you want to rotate. Select the Rotate option.

Type Mask Tools

In essence, use the Type Mask tools to create very complex selections – selections in the shape of type. This can be powerful and flexible when you want to show images through the shape of letterforms.

Because you do not get a preview of type settings in the image window when you use the Type Mask tool, create a standard type layer with the type settings you want before you use the Type Mask tool. Settings you create for the standard layer in the Type Tool dialogue box are remembered. Delete the standard type layer afterwards.

1 Select the Type Mask tool. Position your cursor on the image where you want the type to start. Click. This sets the text insertion point. The Type Tool dialogue box appears. Create settings for Font and Style, Size and Leading as for standard type.

2 OK the dialogue box. A type selection appears in the image window. With the Type Mask tool still selected, position your cursor inside the selection border, then click and drag to reposition

the selection area if necessary. Notice that the Type Mask tool does not create a new layer.

3 You can now drag the selection to a new image window, create a new layer from the selection (see page 124), or use any commands that you would typically use on a selection.

Type and Layer Effects

Layer Effects can be applied to type layers whilst the type layer remains an editable-type layer.

1 To apply a Layer Effect to a type layer, first click on a type layer to make it active.

2 Choose a layer effect using the Effects sub-menu. Notice that the layer in the layers palette now has a [T] and an [f] icon indicating that it is an editable type layer with a layer effect applied. (See page 121 for information on working with layer effects. See page 132 for information on working with editable type layers.)

The editable type layer with its layer effect separated from the Background layer.

Yemen

Paths

An understanding of paths in Photoshop is essential for creating cut-outs for use in page layout applications such as QuarkXPress and Adobe PageMaker.

You can save paths with the image file in Photoshop format, convert paths into selections, or convert selections into paths. You can also export paths to Adobe Illustrator.

Covers

Converting Selections to Paths | 146

Creating Paths Using the Pen Tool | 148

Showing and Selecting Paths and Points | 150

Adding, Deleting and Converting Points | 151

Creating Corner Points | 152

Editing Points | 153

Exporting Clipping Paths | 154

Exporting Paths to Adobe Illustrator | 156

Chapter Eleven

Converting Selections to Paths

A quick and convenient technique for creating a path is to make a selection, convert the selection into a work path, and then into a path.

Use Window > Show Paths to show the Paths palette.

1 First make a selection using any of the selection tools. Then, use the Paths palette pop-up menu and choose Make Work Path, or click the Make Work Path icon.

You can only have one work path in the Paths palette at any one time. A work path is a temporary path only. For a path to be saved when you save your file, you must first save the path (see step 4, page 147).

2 The Make Work Path dialogue box appears if you use the Make Work Path command. Specify a tolerance value (from 0.5–10). (If you click the Make Work Path icon, the last-used settings from the dialogue box are applied automatically.) The tolerance value controls how closely the path conforms to the selection. A low tolerance value creates a path that follows the selection tightly, but creates a greater number of points. A high tolerance value produces a path that follows the selection more loosely, but with fewer points.

3 OK the dialogue box. A work path appears in the Paths palette, along with a thumbnail of the path.

4 Choose Save Path from the pop-up menu if you want to save this path before

making any adjustments to it. Enter a name. OK the dialogue box. The new path appears in the palette, replacing the work path.

5 To hide the path, click in empty space in the Paths palette, or choose Turn Off Path from the pop-up menu. To show the path, click on the path name to select it. The path highlights.

Click in an empty area of the Paths palette to turn off the path, leaving the selection marquee only visible in the image window.

Converting Paths to Selections

You can also convert a path into a selection. This is useful when you want a very accurate selection.

To convert a path into a selection, click on the path in the Paths palette to highlight it. Then choose Make Selection from the pop-up menu, or click the Make Selection icon.

Creating Paths Using the Pen Tool

You can use the Pen tool to create paths. When you start to create a path it appears as a 'work path' in the Paths palette. A work path is only a temporary path.

The Pen tool creates anchor points which are connected by straight lines or curved segments. You can use the other tools in the Paths tool group to modify a path by adding, deleting or moving anchor points, and by changing the nature of the point, from smooth to corner and vice versa. You can also edit curved segments by dragging the Bezier direction points.

1 To create a path, double-click the Pen tool in the Toolbox to display the Pen Tool Options palette if it is not already showing. You can select the Rubber band option if you want to see a preview of the line segments as you draw.

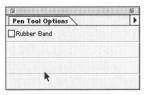

2 Position your cursor where you want to start drawing the path, then click, release the button, move the mouse and click again to create a straight line segment. Continue moving your cursor and clicking to create further straight line segments.

You can press the Delete key to delete the last anchor point. If you press Delete twice, you will delete the entire path.

3   Alternatively, you can click and drag to set an anchor point and create direction lines for a curve segment.

4   Then, release the button and move the cursor, and again click and drag to create the next anchor point with direction lines.

5   Continue in this way to create the path you want.

You can only have one work path in a file. It is a good idea to save the path and give it a name, so you do not delete it accidentally by creating another work path. See pages 146–147 for details on saving your work path.

6   Position the Pen tool cursor at the start point. Notice the cursor now has a small circle attached to it. Click to create a closed path. The path will appear in the Paths palette with the default title of Work Path.

7   To create an open path, follow the techniques outlined above, but instead of clicking back at the start point, click on the Pen tool in the Toolbox to finish the path. This is now an open path to which you could, for example, apply a stroke.

Showing and Selecting Paths and Points

Use the following techniques for selecting, deselecting and deleting paths.

1 To select a path, first you have to show it. To do this, click the path name in the Paths palette. The path now shows in the image window.

2 To select the path, select the Direct Selection tool (the hollow arrow). If necessary, click on the path to make it active. You will now see the curve and line segments together with the anchor points.

A selected anchor point is a solid square; a non-selected point is a hollow square.

3 Click on the anchor point of a curve segment to select the point and display the direction points.

4 To select and move an entire path, follow step 1 above, then hold down alt/Option (Mac) or Alt (Windows) and click on the path. Using the Direct Selection tool, position your cursor on an anchor point or curve segment, then click and drag to reposition the path. To deselect a path, click away from the path using the Direct Selection tool.

To improve the clarity of these screen shots, the path has been moved 1 pixel away from the edge of the image.

5 To delete a path, with a point or line segment of the path selected, press the Delete key twice. Alternatively, with the entire path selected, press the Delete key once. You can also drag the path name onto the Wastebasket icon in the Paths palette.

Adding, Deleting and Converting Points

You often need to add points and delete points on a path.

1   To add a point, make sure the path is selected, select the Add Point tool from the Pen Tool group, position your cursor on the path and then click. If you click on a curve segment you automatically get an anchor point with direction points. If you click on a straight line segment, you get just an anchor point.

For a smooth point, when you drag one of the direction points, the other point balances it to maintain a smooth curve at the anchor point.

2   To delete a point, make sure the path is selected, select the Delete Point tool, position your cursor on an existing anchor point, then click. The path redraws without the point.

3   To convert a smooth point into a corner point, select the Convert Anchor Point tool, position your cursor on a direction point, then click and drag. Use the Direct Selection tool to make any further changes to the direction points.

A corner point is one which allows a sharp change of direction at the anchor point. Notice that for a corner point, when you drag one of the direction points, the other point is not affected. You have complete, independent control over each direction point.

4   To convert anchor points on straight line segments into smooth points, select the Convert Anchor Point tool, position your cursor on the anchor point, then click and drag. Direction lines appear around the point. Use the Direct Selection tool to make any further changes to the points.

5   To convert a smooth point into a corner point without direction lines, select the Convert Anchor Point tool, then click on an anchor point.

Creating Corner Points

As you use the Pen tool to create paths, you can draw corner points as you go, in combination with straight line segments and smooth points. In many instances, a smooth point cannot create the shape of the path you want.

A corner point allows a sharp change of direction at the anchor point. In a corner point, the direction points can be manipulated independently. This is what makes them essential to create paths that require sharp changes of direction.

The paths in these screen shots have been moved one pixel away from the edge of the leaf so that they display more clearly. When you create a clipping path, it is best to position the path a pixel or so inside the shape you want to cut out, to avoid unwanted edge pixels being included. Unwanted edge pixels are sometimes referred to as 'edge tear'.

1 To draw a corner point, click and drag as you would to set a smooth point. Concentrate on getting the shape of the path coming into the point correct. Release the mouse button.

2 Position your cursor on the anchor point, hold down alt/Alt, then click and drag off the point. This converts the point to a corner point. You are now controlling the direction of the outgoing curve segment. As you drag the second direction point, notice that it no longer has any effect on the incoming direction point.

3 Move your cursor, then continue drawing either smooth or corner points.

Editing Points

Paths invariably need to be modified and fine-tuned to produce the result you require.

Select the Direct Selection tool to edit paths and points (see page 150, 'Showing and Selecting Paths and Points').

1 To edit a smooth point, make sure the path is selected, then click on the anchor point to select it. Direction points appear either side of the anchor point. Direction points control the shape and length of a curve segment.

Select an anchor point and press the arrow keys to move the selected point in 1-pixel increments.

2 When you drag a direction point of a smooth anchor point, as you change the angle of one side, the other direction point moves to balance the point you are moving. This ensures the curve is always smooth through the anchor point.

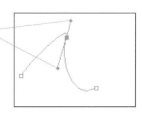

3 The further away from the anchor point you drag a direction point, the longer the associated curve segment becomes. As the curve segment is anchored at the anchor points at either end, this causes the curve segment to bow out more. Bring the direction point closer to the anchor point and the curve segment becomes shorter.

4 When you drag direction points on a corner anchor point, each moves totally independently of the other, allowing a sharp change of direction at the point.

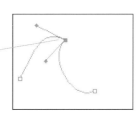

Exporting Clipping Paths

Create a clipping path when you want to create transparent areas in an image that you intend to use in an application such as Adobe Illustrator or QuarkXPress.

A clipping path makes areas of the image outside the path transparent, allowing you to see past the outline of the image to the background on which the image is placed.

Flatness allows a PostScript printer to create less memory-intensive paths at output. If you use too high a flatness value, you get an approximate path that does not accurately conform to the path you created.

For high-resolution printing (1200–2400 dpi) a flatness value of 8 to 10 should be acceptable. Use a value of 1 to 3 for low resolution printing (300–600 dpi). Leave the field blank to use the printer's default setting.

1   Create a saved path (see page 147). If you have more than one path in the Paths palette, make sure you select the appropriate path. Use the pop-up palette to select Clipping Path.

2   Use the Path pop-up to specify a different path to make into a clipping path if necessary. Enter a flatness value.

3   When you have saved a clipping path, you need to save the file in EPS or TIFF file format for output. Choose File > Save As. In the Save As dialogue box, give the file a name and specify where you want to save it.

4 Choose Photoshop
EPS or TIFF from
the Format pop-up.
Click Save. Clipping

Save this document as:
rowan

Cancel

Save

Format: Photoshop EPS ▾

Paths saved with the image are automatically exported with
the file when you save in Photoshop EPS or TIFF file format.

*Remember to
convert the file
to an
appropriate
mode – e.g.
CMYK – before you save the
file in EPS format.*

5 When you import
the file into a
QuarkXPress
page, the clipping
path hides areas of
the image outside
the clipping path.
The second
version of the
same image on
this Quark page
has a white
background and
does not have a
clipping path.

*Select a TIFF
preview option
if you intend to
use the image
on the
Windows platform.*

Exporting Paths to Adobe Illustrator

Exporting a path to Illustrator is useful when you want to place type along a path originated in Photoshop. The type can then be saved as an EPS file in Illustrator and placed back into Photoshop. This is useful because Photoshop does not have as much flexibility for creating type effects as Illustrator.

1 To export a path to Adobe Illustrator, choose File > Export > Paths to Illustrator. In the Export Paths dialogue box, change the name if necessary, but leave the automatically generated .ai extension to distinguish the file. If your Photoshop document has more than one saved path, use the Write pop-up to choose the path you want to export. Click Save.

You can use the Export Paths to Illustrator command and then open the file in Macromedia FreeHand if you do not have Adobe Illustrator.

2 Use File > Open in Adobe Illustrator to import the path and place type along it. Save the Illustrator file in EPS format.

3 Place the Illustrator EPS into the Photoshop document that you originally exported the path from. (See page 45, Chapter Three.)

4 Position the EPS bounding box, resize the EPS if necessary, then press Return/Enter to place the text from Illustrator onto a new layer.

Channels and Masks

The Channels palette stores colour information about an image and can also be used to store selections on a permanent basis.

Masks are created and used in a variety of ways in Photoshop. The basic principle of masks is that you use them to protect areas of an image from editing that you carry out on the unmasked areas of the image.

Use Quick Mask mode when you don't want to save the mask for future use. Layer masks control how different areas of pixels on a layer are hidden or revealed.

Covers

Quick Mask Mode | 158

The Channels Palette | 159

Saving and Loading Selections | 160

Editing Alpha Channel Masks | 162

Layer Masks | 164

Channel and Quick Mask Options | 166

Chapter Twelve

Quick Mask Mode

In Quick Mask mode you create a 50% red, semi-transparent overlay. This overlay represents the protected area of the image. The overlay is similar in concept to a traditional rubylith mask. Quick Mask mode is particularly useful because you can see both the image and the mask as you create and fine-tune the mask.

You can make a rough selection first, then go into Quick Mask mode and edit the mask further if necessary.

1 To create a quick mask, click the Quick Mask Mode icon. Make sure that the default foreground and background colours are black and white respectively.

2 Show the Brushes palette and choose a brush size. Use a hard-edged brush for most control. Select a painting tool and drag across your image to 'paint' in the mask. Painting with black adds to the mask. Although you see through the 50% red mask, the pixels covered by the mask are completely protected.

Painting with grey or any other colour creates a semi-transparent or partial mask.

3 To remove areas from the mask you can use the Eraser tool, or paint with white.

4 When you are satisfied with your mask, click the Standard Mode button. This turns the areas of the image that were not part of your quick mask into a selection. You can now make changes to the selected areas (in this example the Blur filter has been applied), leaving the areas that were the quick mask unchanged.

The Channels Palette

The Channels palette (Window > Show Channels) shows a breakdown of the colour components that combine to make up the composite colour image that you work with most of the time on-screen.

You can change the display of channels from greyscale to the colour they represent by choosing File > Preferences > Display and Cursor. Select Colour Channels in Colour.

For example, in RGB mode, there are four channels – the composite image (all the other channels combined), and then a channel each for the red, green and blue colour components of the image. In CMYK mode, there are five channels.

Using the Channels palette you can be selective about which of the colour components in your image you change.

1 To switch to a specific channel, click the channel name in the Channels palette. The channel highlights to indicate that it is selected. The image window changes according to the channel you chose.

Indexed Colour mode, Greyscale mode and Bitmap mode all have only one channel.

2 You can view additional channels by clicking the eye icon for a channel. The image window changes, but your editing remains limited to the selected channel.

3 Click on the composite channel to return to normal image-editing view.

Saving and Loading Selections

Because you can only have one 'active' selection in an image at any one time, the facility to store a selection which can be reloaded later is vital, especially if the selection is complex and took some time to create. You save selections as an extra channel in the Channels palette. These extra channels are referred to as 'alpha channels'.

An alpha channel is an 8-bit greyscale channel, which means that every time you save a selection as a channel, you are adding to the file size of your image.

Saving Selections

1 To save a selection to a channel, make your selection on the image, then choose Select > Save Selection. The Save Selection dialogue box appears. Specify in which document you wish to save the channel. (You can save channels in another document to keep the file size of the current document as small as possible.) Leave the Channel pop-up on New. Enter a name for the channel. Click OK. Alternatively, make your selection and then click the Save Selection icon in the Channels palette.

You can only save an alpha channel with a picture in Photoshop, TIFF or PICT (RGB) file formats.

2 In the Channels palette, you will see an extra channel. This is the new 'alpha channel'. An alpha channel is a greyscale channel.

3 When you have saved a selection to an alpha channel you can freely deselect the selection in your image, as you can now reselect exactly the same area at any time using the alpha channel.

...cont'd

Loading Selections

Use the following process to re-select an area using the alpha channel:

1 To load a channel selection as a selection on the image, make sure the composite image is displayed. You can do this by clicking on the topmost channel name in the Channels palette. Then choose Select > Load Selection. The Load Selection dialogue box appears.

2 Use the Channel pop-up menu to specify which channel you want to load. Select an operation as appropriate. The operations allow you to control how the selection you are about to load interacts with any existing selection in the image – adding to it, subtracting from it or intersecting with it. Click OK.

When you are working in Quick Mask mode, you can turn the quick mask into an alpha channel by dragging the quick mask entry that appears in the Channels palette onto the New Channel icon.

3 Alternatively, using the Channels palette, drag the channel you want to load onto the Load Selection icon.

4 To delete a channel, drag the channel name onto the Wastebasket icon at the bottom of the palette.

Editing Alpha Channel Masks

You can display an alpha channel without loading it onto the image as a selection. You can then edit the mask by painting with black, white or grey.

1 To display an alpha channel, choose Windows > Show Channels to display the Channels palette. Click on the alpha channel you want to display. The channel name turns grey, and an eye icon in the left column of the palette indicates that this is the visible channel.

2 The image window changes from the composite view to a greyscale representation of the mask. The white area represents the selection and the black portions represent the protected areas.

If you paint with grey you can create a semi-transparent mask.

3 To edit a selection channel, select a painting tool and brush size. Click the Default Colours icon if necessary, to change the foreground colour to black. Paint with black to remove areas from the selection. Paint with white on any black portion of the mask to add it to the selection.

Make sure you do not have a selection showing (marching ants) before you attempt to modify or edit the selection mask channel.

Another useful technique for editing a selection mask is to view a mask and image simultaneously by turning the alpha channel selection into a coloured mask (very much like using Quick Mask mode) and then reshaping the mask by painting with black, white or shades of grey.

1 To reshape a mask, make sure you don't have an active selection on your image. Click on the alpha channel in the Channels palette to select it. It highlights, and the eye icon shows on the left. The image window now displays the greyscale selection channel mask. Notice that the eye icon disappears from the Composite RGB channel as well as from the individual Red, Green and Blue channels.

Typically, when you edit masks, you will paint with black or white, with the mode set to Normal and an opacity of 100%. However, you can reduce the opacity or pressure setting in order to create a partial mask.

2 Click into the currently empty eye icon position for the Composite channel. The eye icon appears for the Composite channel, as well as in the individual Red, Green and Blue channels. The Composite channel now also shows in the image window. However, only the alpha channel is selected – indicated by the highlight.

3 The image window now changes in appearance. The selection mask area appears as normal, whilst the protected or masked portions of the image have a quick mask-type transparent film applied.

Make sure that the eye icon for an alpha channel mask is not selected, then click the Composite channel when you want to return to the standard editing view.

4 Select the paintbrush or pencil tool. Paint with white to remove areas of the image from the mask, in other words to enlarge the unmasked area. Paint with black to add portions of the image to the mask.

Layer Masks

Use layer masks to hide or reveal areas of a layer. A layer mask is extremely useful because you can use it to try out effects without actually changing the pixels on the layer. When you have achieved the result you want, you can apply the mask as a permanent change. If you are not satisfied, you can discard the mask without having permanently affected the pixels on the layer.

For information on creating layers, see Chapter Nine. For information on using filters, see Chapter Fourteen.

This example begins with an image with two layers. The background layer is the original scan; the other layer was created using the Render > Clouds filter.

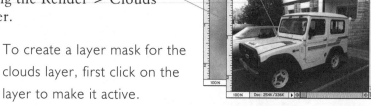

1 To create a layer mask for the clouds layer, first click on the layer to make it active.

Choose Layer > Add Layer Mask > Reveal All. Reveal All means that all the pixels in the layer are visible. The Clouds layer now completely obscures the background layer.

You can only have one layer mask per layer.

2 In the Layers palette, the layer mask is active, indicated by the mask icon next to the eye icon. Click on the layer thumbnail to make the layer active (the paintbrush icon indicates that you can now work directly on the layer). Click on the layer mask icon to continue editing the mask.

3 With the layer mask selected, make sure that the foreground colour is set to black. Choose a painting tool and start painting. Painting with black hides pixels on the clouds layer, revealing pixels on the Background layer.

4 Pixels on the clouds layer are not permanently erased when you paint with black. Paint with white to show pixels on the clouds layer – in effect hiding pixels on the background layer. (If you choose Layer > Add Layer Mask > Hide All, you start with the opposite scenario to the above. Now all the pixels on the clouds layer are hidden. Paint with white to reveal pixels on the clouds layer, paint with black to hide them.)

You can paint with shades of grey to partially hide pixels on the clouds layer.

5 To temporarily switch off the Layer mask, choose Layer > Disable Mask, or hold down Shift, then click on the Layer Mask icon. To reactivate the mask, choose Layer > Enable Layer Mask, or hold down Shift, then click again on the Layer Mask icon.

6 To apply the layer mask as a permanent change, choose Layer > Remove Layer Mask, or drag the Layer Mask icon onto the Wastebasket icon in the bottom of the palette.

7 Click Apply. Once you apply a layer mask you lose the flexibility of making further changes – the effect is fixed. Click discard only if you want to delete the mask.

Channel and Quick Mask Options

The Channel Options dialogue box and the Quick Mask Options dialogue box allow you to control the colour of a mask and whether the protected or unprotected area of the image is coloured with the overlay.

1 To change channel options, double-click the alpha channel name. Alternatively, with the alpha channel selected, use the Channels pop-up menu to choose Channel Options.

2 In the Channel Options dialogue box you can enter a new name for the channel. You can also choose Selected Areas to reverse the way in which the colour will apply. In other words, masked (protected) areas will appear white, while the selection area (unprotected) will appear black.

3 To change the colour used to represent the masked (protected) area and its opacity, click the Colour box and choose a new colour from the colour picker.

4 To change the settings for a quick mask, double-click either the Quick Mask Mode icon or the Standard Mode icon, then make the appropriate changes in the dialogue box that appears.

Colour Correction Techniques

Colour correction involves making changes to the overall brightness and contrast in an image and also the colour balance to compensate for any tonal deficiencies and colour casts in the original scan.

You should bear in mind that although colour corrections can improve the overall appearance of an image, inevitably some colour values will be lost – certain pixels in the original scan that were different colours will end up remapped to the same colour.

Covers

The Brightness/Contrast Command | 168

The Auto Levels Command | 169

The Levels Dialogue Box | 170

The Curves Dialogue Box | 172

The Colour Balance Dialogue Box | 174

Chapter Thirteen

The Brightness/Contrast Command

The Brightness/Contrast command provides the least complicated controls for changing overall brightness and contrast levels in an image. It does not allow you to make changes to individual colour channels.

1 To change brightness and contrast, choose Image > Adjust > Brightness/Contrast.

2 Drag the Brightness and Contrast sliders to the right or left, or enter a value in the entry boxes (-100 to +100). OK the dialogue box.

Choose Image > Adjust > Auto Contrast (Ctrl/Command +Alt+Shift+L) to automatically adjust the contrast in the image. Highlights should appear lighter and shadows darker resulting in an overall improvement in the image.

3 If you are making adjustments to a selection, click the Preview button to see, on-screen, the result of the settings you choose.

The Auto Levels Command

Auto Levels allows you to adjust brightness and contrast automatically. Auto Levels examines each colour channel independently and changes the darkest pixels to black and the lightest pixels to white, then redistributes the remaining shades of grey between these two points.

Auto Levels works best on images that have a reasonably even distribution of tonal values throughout the image, as it redistributes pixels based on white and black points, with a tendency to increase contrast. This generally produces good results, but Auto Levels does not allow the precision of manual adjustments that you can make using the Levels and Curves dialogue boxes.

1 To apply Auto Levels to an image, choose Image > Adjust > Auto Levels. (Use Edit > Undo if you do not like the result.)

2 You can also use the Auto Levels command from within the Levels and Curves dialogue boxes. Click the Auto button.

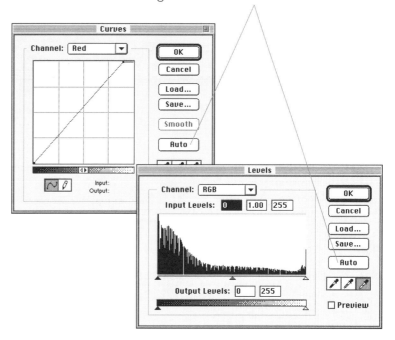

The Levels Dialogue Box

Use the Levels dialogue box (Image > Adjust > Levels) to adjust the tonal balance for colour and greyscale images. You can adjust highlight, shadow and midtone ranges for a selection or an entire image, or you can make changes to individual channels only.

Input Levels

The Input Level sliders and entry boxes allow you to improve the contrast in a 'flat' image.

The most flexible way of working with Levels, Curves and Colour Balance is to set up Adjustment layers. Adjustment layers allow you to readjust settings in the respective dialogue boxes until you are satisfied with the result. (See page 121.)

1 Use the Channel pop-up menu to select a channel. If you do not select an individual channel, you work on the composite image and affect all channels.

2 To darken an image, drag the solid black slider to the right. Alternatively, enter an appropriate value in the leftmost Input Levels entry box. This maps or clips pixels to black. For example, if you drag the black slider to 15, all pixels with an original value between 0 and 15 become black. The result is a darker image.

Dragging either or both the black or white sliders inwards has the effect of increasing contrast in the image.

3 To lighten an image, drag the hollow, white Input Levels slider to the left. Alternatively, enter an appropriate value in the rightmost Input Levels entry box. The result is to map or clip pixels to white. For example, if you drag the white slider to 245, all pixels with an original value between 245 and 255 become white. The result is a lighter image.

Gamma

The grey triangle and the middle Input Levels entry box control the Gamma value in the image. The Gamma value is the brightness level of mid-grey pixels in the image.

When you OK the Levels dialogue box, you can use Edit > Undo/ Redo a number of times to evaluate the changes.

1 To lighten midtones, drag the grey slider to the left, or increase the Gamma value in the Input Levels entry box above the default setting of 1.00.

2 To darken midtones, drag the grey slider to the right, or decrease the Gamma value in the Input Levels entry box.

Output Levels

You can use the Output Levels entry boxes or sliders to decrease the amount of contrast in an image.

1 Drag the black Output Levels slider to the right to lighten the image and reduce the contrast.

See page 161 for an explanation of Auto Levels and the Auto button.

2 Drag the white Output Levels slider to the left to darken the image and reduce the contrast.

The Curves Dialogue Box

The Curves dialogue box (Image > Adjust > Curves) offers the most versatile set of controls for making tonal adjustments in an image. The central brightness graph in the dialogue box displays the original and adjusted brightness values for pixels in the image. The graph is a straight line from 0 (black) to 255 (white), before any adjustments are made – input and output values for pixels are the same.

You should be careful not to click on the brightness bar at the bottom of the Curves dialogue box accidentally.

The default brightness bar starts black and graduates to white. In this state, the brightness curve indicates the brightness values of colours in the image; the brightness curve starts at 0, for black, and moves to 255, for white.

The horizontal axis of the graph represents the original or input values, the vertical axis represents the output or adjusted values. By adjusting the brightness curve, you are remapping the brightness values of pixels in the image.

| To add a point to the curve, select the Point tool. (This is the default selection.) Click on the curve. (You can add up to fifteen points.) Drag the point(s) around to edit the curve. Alternatively, click at a point in the graph and the curve will change according to where you clicked.

2 To delete a point, click on a point to select it, then press the Delete/Backspace key. You can also drag it outside the Brightness graph.

3 To lighten an image, select the Point tool, position your cursor near the midpoint of the graph, then click to place a new point. Click and drag this point upwards.

...cont'd

Hold down alt/ Alt, then click on the Reset button (previously Cancel) to restore the original settings in the dialogue box.

4 To darken an image, select the Point tool, position your cursor near the midpoint of the graph, then click to place a point. Drag the point downwards.

5 To increase the contrast in an image, place a point at roughly the ¼ tone part of the graph and drag this upwards to lighten the highlights. Next, place a point at roughly the ¾ tone part of the graph. Drag this downward to darken the shadow areas. The result is to increase the contrast in the image by lightening the highlights and darkening the shadows, whilst leaving the midtones more or less untouched.

6 Reverse the setting in step 5 to decrease the contrast in an image.

7 To limit changes to the midtones and highlights, click on the graph to place a point at the ¾ tones. Place a point at the ¼ tones and drag this upwards. Reverse this procedure to change midtones and shadows without affecting highlights.

The Colour Balance Dialogue Box

Like the Brightness/Contrast command, the Colour Balance dialogue box provides general controls for correcting an overall colour cast in an image. As such, it provides the least complex method of colour correction.

The Colour Balance dialogue box works on the principle of complimentary colours. If there is too much cyan in an image, you drag the Cyan–Red slider towards red to remove the cyan colour cast. If there is too much magenta, drag the Magenta–Green slider towards green.

Work on the composite view of an image when using the Colour Balance dialogue box.

1 To adjust the colour balance of an image, choose Image > Adjust > Colour Balance. Click the Shadow, Midtone or Highlights radio button to specify the tonal range to which you want to make changes.

2 Drag the colour sliders to reduce/increase the amount of a colour in the image.

Preserve Luminosity
Select this option to prevent brightness values from changing as you change colour levels. This helps maintain the overall colour balance in the image.

Filters

Photoshop ships with more than 95 filters as standard. Filters add enormous creative flexibility and potential to image-manipulation, and they are well worth experimenting with.

You can use filters across an entire image, or you can apply them to selections to limit the results to specific areas. Filters cannot be applied to images in Bitmap or Indexed Colour mode.

Covers

Filter Controls | 176

Unsharp Mask and Sharpen Filters | 177

Blur Filters | 179

Noise Filters | 181

Filter Samples | 183

Chapter Fourteen

Filter Controls

Many of the filters have standard controls, which are explained below.

1 Click the Preview check box to see the effect of your settings previewed in the main image window, as well as in the Preview window inside the filter dialogue box.

2 Click and drag on the image in the Preview window to scroll around to preview different parts of the image. Alternatively, with the filter dialogue box active, position your cursor in the main image window – the cursor becomes a hollow box – then click to set the view in the Preview window.

Unsharp Mask

OK

Cancel

☒ Preview

⊞ 100% ⊟

Amount: 96 %

Radius: 1.0 pixels

Threshold: 10 levels

3 Click the '+' or '–' buttons to zoom in or out on areas of the image. You can also use the Command + Spacebar (Mac) or Ctrl + Spacebar (Windows) keyboard shortcuts within the Preview window or the image window.

4 Hold down alt/Alt and click the Reset button (previously Cancel) to revert to the original settings in the dialogue box.

5 After you OK a filter dialogue box, use Command + F (Mac) or Ctrl + F (Windows) to reapply the last-used filter and its settings.

A line flashing under the Preview check box means that Photoshop is still rendering the new settings.

Unsharp Mask and Sharpen Filters

These filters allow you to enhance the detail of your images.

Unsharp Mask

This is a powerful function which can help you to sharpen blurry images in specific areas. For example, if you rotate an image, or change the dimensions or resolution of the image, it may blur due to any interpolation that Photoshop applies. This can also happen when you convert from RGB to CMYK. Where the Unsharp Mask filter finds edges (areas where there is a high degree of contrast), it increases the contrast between adjacent pixels. The result is to create an apparent improvement in the focus of the image.

1 To use Unsharp Mask to sharpen an image, choose Filter > Sharpen > Unsharp mask. The Unsharp Mask dialogue box appears.

2 Adjust settings for Amount, Radius and Threshold. Click OK or press Return/Enter.

Amount – Use this to control the amount of sharpening applied to the edges (minimum = 1, maximum = 500). The picture will become pixellated if the amount is too high.

Values below 50% produce subtle effects; values between 50% and 250% produce moderate results, while values between 300% and 500% produce dramatic, exaggerated results.

The settings for Radius and Threshold need to be taken into account when setting the amount value (see the next page).

Radius – Radius controls the depth of pixels along the high-contrast edges that are changed.

A low radius value restricts the impact of the filter; higher values distribute the impact. Radius values of 2.0 or lower usually produce acceptable sharpening.

Threshold – Sets a level for the minimum amount of contrast between pixels an area must have before it will be modified. The Threshold value is the difference between two adjacent pixels – as measured in brightness levels – that must occur for Photoshop to recognise them as an edge.

High threshold values limit changes to areas where there is a high degree of colour difference. Use low values to apply the filter more generally throughout the image.

On high-resolution images, use a Threshold value of 10 or higher to apply the sharpening effect to specific areas only.

Sharpen and Sharpen More

Use the Sharpen and Sharpen More filters when an image becomes blurred after resampling. Both filters work by increasing contrast between adjacent pixels throughout the image or selection. Sharpen More has a more pronounced effect than Sharpen.

Sharpen Edges

This filter has a more specific effect, applying sharpening along high-contrast edges. In effect, it has a less global impact on a selection or image than Sharpen and Sharpen More.

Blur Filters

The Blur filters reduce the contrast between adjacent pixels along edges where considerable colour shifts occur, to create a softening, defocusing effect. Blurring produces the opposite effect to sharpening – which increases the contrast between adjacent pixels.

Blur More produces an effect roughly 3 times stronger than the Blur filter.

'Blur' and 'Blur More' blur a selection in preset amounts offering only a limited degree of control. For greater control when blurring you can use the Gaussian Blur option, which blurs according to a bell-shaped Gaussian distribution curve.

To Blur a Layer or Selection

Create a selection if you want to limit the effect of the Blur filter to a specific area of your image. Choose Filter > Blur > Blur, or Filter > Blur > Blur More.

Motion Blur

You can use Motion Blur to create the effect of a moving subject or camera.

1. To create a motion blur, make a selection, if required. Choose Filter > Blur > Motion Blur.

Angle = 0,
Distance = 12

2. Enter a value in the Angle box, or drag the Angle indicator to specify the angle or direction of the blur.

Enter a value in the Distance entry box to specify the distance in pixels for the blur effect. OK the dialogue box.

Angle = -45,
Distance = 12

Angle = -53,
Distance = 26

Radial Blur

Radial Blur creates the effect of zooming in as you take a picture.

If you are working on a layer, make sure that Preserve Transparency is deselected for the blur to take effect.

1 To create a radial blur, make a selection if required. Choose Filter > Blur > Radial Blur.

2 Select a Blur Method and Quality, and specify an Amount (0–100). Click and drag in the Blur Centre window to specify the centre point for the zoom or spin effect. OK the dialogue box.

Amount – This value determines the distance pixels are moved to create the blur effect. Higher values produce more intense effects.

Zoom – Choose Zoom to create a zoom-like blurring effect.

Spin – Spin rotates and blurs pixels around a central point.

Quality – Good and Best produce better, smoother results due to the interpolation methods used, but take longer.

Noise Filters

Add Noise

The Add Noise filter randomly distributes high-contrast pixels in an image, creating a grainy effect.

To add noise, create a selection, or work on the entire image. Choose Filter > Noise > Add Noise. Specify Amount, Distribution and Monochromatic options.

Amount – Determines the degree to which pixels are changed from their original colour. Enter a number from 1–999.

You can use Add Noise to reduce banding in graduated fills.

Uniform – Produces an even spread of pixels.

Gaussian – Produces a more dramatic result.

Monochromatic – Choose Monochromatic to distribute greyscale dots.

Add Noise is a good way to begin creating textured backgrounds.

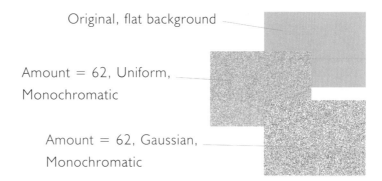

Original, flat background

Amount = 62, Uniform, Monochromatic

Amount = 62, Gaussian, Monochromatic

Dust & Scratches

Use the Dust & Scratches filter to remove small imperfections and blemishes in a scan caused by dust, scratches. The degree of success you have with this filter depends very much on the image or selection to which you apply it.

Radius and Threshold settings are interdependent, and both are taken into account before changes are made.

To remove dust and scratches, create a selection or work on the entire image. Choose Filters > Noise > Dust & Scratches. Specify Radius and Threshold settings. Click OK.

Radius – Determines how small a blemish must be for it to be worked upon by the filter. For example, at a radius of 3 pixels, the Dust & Scratches filter will not attempt to make changes to imperfections above this size.

Threshold – Specifies the minimum amount of contrast between pixels there must be before changes are made.

Despeckle Filter

This produces the opposite effect to Add Noise, smoothing and blurring the image, but having little effect on edges.

Median Filter

The Median filter also removes noise from a poor-quality scan. It works by averaging the colour of adjacent pixels in an image.

To use the Median filter, create a selection, or work on the entire image. Choose Filter > Noise > Median. Specify a Radius value (1–16). OK the dialogue box.

Filter Samples

The following examples of filters provide only a sample of the complete range of filters available in the Filter menu.

Original

Use Command + F (Mac) or Ctrl + F (Windows) to reapply the last-used filter and settings.

Artistic

Coloured Pencil   Cut Out

Dry Brush   Film Grain

Brush Strokes

Accented   Angled
Edges   Strokes

It is well worth making a copy of your image to work on before you start experimenting with filters.

Cross Hatch   Dark Strokes

Distort

Diffuse Glow   Glass

Ocean Ripple   Pinch

Pixellate

Colour
Halftone   Crystallise

Choose Filter > Fade... to reduce the effect of a filter on an image.

Facet   Fragment

Render

          Difference
Clouds   Clouds

Lens Flare   Lighting Effects

Original

Sketch

Bas Relief   Chalk and
                      Charcoal

Charcoal   Chrome

Stylise

Diffuse   Emboss

Extrude   Find Edges

Texture

Craquelure   Grain

Mosaic Tiles   Patchwork

Other

Custom   High Pass

Maximum   Minimum

Artistic

Fresco   Neon Glow

Paint Daubs   Palette Knife

Web and Multimedia Images

The success of the World Wide Web is in no small part due to its ability to include images in HTML pages. This section looks at some of the considerations for using different image types effectively in formats suited to the environment of the WWW. It also covers using images for multimedia work.

Balancing file size and image quality is a primary concern when creating images for Web and multimedia use. Generally, the smaller the file size, the quicker the image will load and display on screen. The following techniques examine ways of reducing file size without losing too much image quality.

An image resolution of 72 ppi is usually satisfactory for images intended for screen-based presentations.

Covers

Save for Web: 2-Up | 186

Optimisation: 4-Up View | 188

Preview and Save Optimised Images | 190

Indexed Colour Mode | 192

Colour Palettes | 193

Dithering | 195

Saving Indexed Colour Images as GIFs | 196

Exporting RGB Images in GIF Format | 197

JPEG Format for Web Images | 199

PNG File Format | 200

Chapter Fifteen

Save for Web – 2Up

The Save for Web command offers comprehensive controls for saving images to be used on the World Wide Web. Use the Save for Web command when you want to create an image that is as small as possible – to ensure the fastest possible download times – without sacrificing too much quality.

Click the 4-Up tab to display versions of the original image, the image using the current optimisation settings, and two other, lower quality variations of the original image, based on the current optimisation settings. (See pages 188 for further details.)

1. Choose File > Save to save any changes you have made to the image in the current file format. Then choose File > Save for Web (Ctrl/Command+Alt+Shift+S).

2. In the Save for Web dialogue box, click the 2-Up tab to compare the original image and the image with optimisation settings applied. Click the Original tab to view only the original Photoshop image. Click the Optimised tab to view the image with optimisation settings applied. When viewing 2-Up and 4-Up, each optimised pane indicates file format, size, and approximate download time for a specific modem speed in the annotations area.

> JPEG
> 2.912K
> 2 sec @ 28.8Kbps
> 10 quality

Use the Zoom and Hand tools as you would in the normal image window to zoom in and out and to scroll to different parts of the image.

3 In 2-Up view, make sure the Optimised pane is selected – indicated by a black border. In the Optimise panel, choose an optimisation level from the presets in the Settings pop-up. The Optimised image pane updates so that you can evaluate different options. GIF, JPEG and PNG file formats are discussed later in this chapter.

To select a pane click into it. A selected pane is indicated by a black highlihgt border around the edge.

4 Use the Preview menu to change the downlaod time readout to that expected for a particular modem speed. The readout updates in the annotation area of the optimised preview panes accordingly.

On Macintosh computers running OS8.6 and later the Save as dialogue box is the updated version.

5 Click the OK button when you are satisfied with your settings for the Optimised image. Specify a location and file name using standard Macintosh/ Windows techniques. (See page 190 for further inforamtion on saving optimised files.)

Optimisation: 4-Up View

The Save for Web dialogue box, with the 4-Up tab selected, is particularly useful because it allows you to preview images using a variety of optimisation levels before you decide which level of optimisation you want.

1 Click the 4-Up tab to view the Original image, the image optimised using the current optimisation settings set in the Optimisation panel, and two lower quality variations of the current optimisation settings.

Use the Zoom and Hand tools to change the magnification and to scroll through images in the preview panes.

2 To change the settings for the Optimised image, click on the Optimised image pane to make sure it is selected. (The typical position for the Optimised image is top right corner of the 4-Up panes.) Choose a new optimisation setting from the presets in the Settings pop-up. The Optimised image pane refreshes to display the results of the new settings.

The Repopulate command treats the selected pane as the Optimised image, then repopulates the 2 remaining comparison panes with lower quality versions of the optimisation settings.

3 Choose Repopulate views from the Optimisation pop-up to update the remaining panes with lower quality optimisation settings.

4 To use one of the lower quality comparison panes as the optimised image, click inside one of the panes to select it. A black highlight border on the pane indicates that it is selected.

For JPEG compression, use a small Blur value, e.g. 0.1 to 0.5 to blur pattern artifacts that may appear along sharp edges. Higher values may reduce image detail noticeably.

5 Choose Repopulate Views from the Optimisation panel pop-up. The selected pane becomes the Optimised image and typically appears in the top right corner. Its optimisation settings appear in the Optimisation area. The comparison panes update with lower quality optimisation settings.

6 To compare different optimisation settings, click on a comparison pane to select it, then choose an optimisation setting from the Settings pop-up. In this case, make sure you do not use the Repopulate Views command.

Preview and Save Optimised Images

You can preview an optimised image in a Web browser before you make a final decision on which optimisation settings to save. This can be a useful check before committing yourself to saving the file.

1 Choose a browser from the Preview pop-up. The browser launches and displays the image from the selected pane. Image details such as file format, dimensions and file size are listed below the image. Below the image details is the HTML code necessary to display the image.

2 To save an optimised image, make sure you select the pane with the settings you want to use. Click OK in the Save for Web dialogue box.

3 Use standard Macintosh/ Windows techniques to navigate to the folder in which you want to save the image. Enter a file name for

the image. The file extension for the optimisation settings is automatically appended to the file name. Make sure you don't delete it. The file is saved using the current settings in the Optimise panel.

The save HTML file option is most useful when saving images from ImageReady with slices.

4 Select the HTML file option to save the HTML code used to display the image as a separate file. This file is automatically named and is saved in the same folder as the optimised image.

Indexed Colour Mode

Indexed Colour mode is an important factor in the preparation of images for use on the World Wide Web and in multimedia applications. It provides an efficient method for reducing the size of a colour image. When you work on RGB colour images in Photoshop, these are typically 24-bit images, capable of displaying over 16 million colours. Indexed Colour Mode converts images to single channel, 8-bit images, capable of displaying a maximum of 256 colours.

Make a selection before you convert to Indexed Colour mode, to weight the colour table towards the colours that occur in the selection.

I   To convert an RGB colour image to Indexed Colour mode, choose Image > Mode > Indexed Colour.

2   Use the Palette pop-up to specify a colour palette which controls and limits the colours that will be used in the image. (See next page.)

When you save a file with an image preview, you increase the size of the file. To save files without a preview, select File > Preferences > Saving Files > Never Save (in the Image Previews pop-up menu).

3   Choose an option from the Forced pop-up to force the inclusion of certain colours in the colour table.

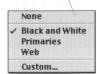

4   Select Transparency to preserve any transparent areas in the image. Deslect Transparency to fill transparent areas with the Matte colour. White is used if there is no Matte colour selected. Matte is only available if there are areas of transparency in the image. (See page 199 for further information.)

5   Set dithering options. (See page 195).

Colour Palettes

A colour palette controls the 256 possible colours that exist in an Indexed Colour image.

Exact

If the image you are converting already has fewer than 256 colours, Exact is the default. The actual number of colours is indicated in the Colours entry box. You cannot dither an Exact palette.

System Palettes

This is the standard, 8-bit system palette of either the Macintosh or Windows system.

Web

This is a palette reduced to 216 colours. Use this palette to achieve consistency across different platforms and when you want to use more than one image on the same Web page. Images which are based on different colour palettes can look artificial when seen side by side.

Uniform

This palette is based on a uniform sampling of colours from the colour spectrum.

Adaptive

This palette is built around the colours that actually occur in an image. For individual images, it gives better results than Web, as the colour table is created by sampling colours from the most frequently occurring areas of the colour spectrum in the image.

Custom

This option takes you into the Colour Table dialogue box and allows you to create your own custom colour table.

Previous

Previous is only available after you have converted an image using either Adaptive or Custom methods. It uses exactly the same palette as created by the previous conversion.

When working with GIF compression settings you can also choose colour palettes from the Palette pop-up in the Optimise area of the Save for Web dialogue box in Photoshop and the Optimise Palette in ImageReady.

Perceptual

The perceptual option creates a colour palette biased towards colours to which the human eye is most sensitive.

Selective

This is similar to Perceptual, but biased towards broad areas of colour in the image and also the preservation of Web colours.

You can specify an exact number of colours for an Indexed Colour image if you don't want the maximum 256 steps. Enter a value in the Colours field.

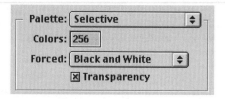

Dithering

Dithering is a technique that simulates colours that are not actually in the colour palette. On computer monitors that support only 256 colours, dithering takes place to simulate a greater range of colours in an image than the monitor is actually capable of displaying. Dithering juxtaposes pixels of different colours to create the illusion of additional colours.

In Photoshop and ImageReady you can choose a dithering method for an image when you optimise it.

1 Choose an option from the Dither pop-up.

2 Set a Dither Amount. Higher values result in more dithering which creates the appearance of a greater number of colours in the image. Higher values can also increase the file size, depending on the image.

Images with areas of solid colour may compress best with Dither set to None. Images with gradients usually need dithering to prevent obvious banding.

3 Select Preserve Exact Colours to protect colours in the colour table from being dithered.

None
No dithering is applied to the image.

Pattern
This creates a square dither pattern, similar to halftones, to simulate colours not available in the colour table.

Diffusion
The result of Diffusion are usually less noticeable than Pattern as the dithering is spread across a range of pixels.

Noise
Applies a random dither pattern. This option can be used for images with slices.

Saving Indexed Colour Images as GIFs

When you have converted an image to Indexed Colour mode, you can then proceed to save the image in GIF format.

This technique works best for flat coloured images such as logos. For photographic type images with subtle colour transitions, JPEG is a better method of preparing images for the World Wide Web.

1 To save the image in GIF format, choose File > Save As. Specify CompuServe GIF from the Format pop-

up menu. Specify a location for saving the file and enter a name. Make sure you use the '.gif' extension. OK the dialogue box.

2 Click the Interlaced option in the GIF Options dialogue box if you want a low-resolution image to download first, followed by progressively more image information as it becomes available from the Web server.

Avoid using GIF format if your image contains a gradient. Use JPEG format instead (see page 199).

Exporting RGB Images in GIF Format

You can use layers to create transparent areas in GIF images, when you export an RGB image in GIF format.

The advantages of converting an RGB image to GIF format are that you can feather the selection you move to a new layer, and that you also have the option to further reduce the number of colours in the GIF file you export.

1 Select the areas of your image that you want to display when the image is downloaded as part of an HTML file.

2 Create a new layer (see Chapter Nine, 'Layers'), then copy the selection to the new, transparent layer.

3 Hide the other layers in the file. (Click on the eye icon in the Layers palette to hide a layer.)

Reducing the number of colours in an image reduces its file size, depending on the size of the image and the original colour content, but you can only specify a reduced number of colours when you export an RGB image to GIF format.

4 Choose File > Export > GIF89a Export.

5 To display transparent areas with a solid colour, you can leave the Transparency Index Colour box as it is. This is the default Web browser grey background colour. Alternatively, click the Transparency Index Colour box and choose a new colour for the transparent areas.

6 Select a palette from the pop-up menu. ──

> Exact
> ✓ Adaptive
> System

7 Use the Preview button to evaluate the result of reducing the number of colours on quality. OK the Preview dialogue box. Change the number of colours if necessary.

8
16
32
64
✓ 128
255
256

GIF89a Export

Zoom Level: 1:1

OK

Zoom Level: 1

8 Select the Interlaced option to specify that the image downloads a low-resolution version which is progressively built up as more information is received from the server.

9 OK the dialogue box to save the file. Make sure you leave the .gif extension in place.

for 15 Web Images ▾   ⬭ 6100HD

JEEP ph
JEEP.gif   Eject
JEEP100ppi ph   Desktop
JEEPred.gif   New ☒

Export to GIF File: Cancel

JEEP ph.gif   Save

JPEG Format for Web Images

For a general introduction to JPEG format, see page 49.

JPEG is a compression format, widely used for preparing images for the World Wide Web. Use JPEG when you are working with photographic-type images, and when preserving colour detail and quality in the image are more important than download time considerations. JPEG does not allow transparency, and file sizes may be larger than for images exported in GIF format, depending on the compression level you choose.

Save images with gradients in JPEG format, as JPEG format produces smaller file sizes than GIFs with an Adaptive palette.

1 To save an image in JPEG format, choose File > Save As. Specify a location, enter a name, then choose JPEG from the Formats pop-up. OK the dialogue box.

2 Choose a colour from the Matte pop-up to simulate background transparency in the image. You need to know the background colour of the Web page, to match the matte colour to it. (Use Save A Copy command to access to be able to access the Matte pop-up.)

JPEG is most suited to compressing continuous-tone images (images in which the distinction between immediately neighbouring pixels is slight). JPEG is not the best format for saving flat colour images.

3 Use the Quality pop-up to specify the amount of compression, or drag the slider. 'Maximum' gives best quality, retaining most of the detail in the image, but least compression. 'Low' gives lowest image quality, but maximum compression.

4 For Format Options, choose Baseline Optimised to optimise the colour quality of the image. Select Progressive and enter a number for Scans to download the image in a series of passes which add detail progressively until the image is completely displayed. Click OK to export the file.

PNG File Format

PNG is a relatively new file format for saving images for use on the Web. There are 2 PNG file format options: PNG-8 and PNG-24.

As a relatively new image file format, not all browsers, especially older browsers, can display images in PNG format.

PNG-8

PNG-8 file format uses 8-bit colour which allows a maximum of 256 colours in an image. It is most effective at compressing areas of solid, flat colour, typically found in line art, logos and illustrations with type.

PNG-8 is a lossless compression formula – no colour information is lost during compression. Depending on the image, PNG-8 compression can produce files 10–30% smaller than the same image compressed using GIF format.

For images which use a very limited range of colours, Gif format can produce smaller file sizes than PNG-8. Use the 4-Up tab when saving images to choose the best optimisation level.

PNG-8 file format can support background transparency and background matting. Background matting enables you to blend the edges of an image into the background colour you set as the background colour of your Web page.

PNG-24

PNG-24 supports 24-bit colour which allows millions of colours in the image. Like JPEG, this is a good format when you want to preserve subtle transitions in tone and colour in a photographic type image.

PNG-24 uses a lossless compression formula – no colour information is discarded during compression. As a result, PNG-24 file sizes are typically larger than if you save the image using JPEG file format.

Multilevel transparency is not supported by all browsers.

PNG-24 supports background transparency and background matting. PNG-24 also supports multilevel transparency which allows greater control over the way in which an image blends into the background colour of a Web page.

Working with Image Ready

With the rapid, commercial development of the World Wide Web, since mid 1990's onward, there has been a growing need for a distinct set of controls and features that allow the user to create eye-catching, optimised images with small file sizes for rapid download times on modems. Creating images for the Web brings a different range of possibilities and technical requirements and constraints when compared with creating images destined to be printed on paper.

ImageReady is designed specifically to meet these rapidly emerging needs. It has dedicated optimization controls, you can create animated GIF files, Slices, Rollovers and background images.

Covers

Photoshop and ImageReady | 202

The ImageReady Toolbox and Image Window | 203

Jumping Between Applications | 204

Creating and Saving Images | 206

Layer Effects in ImageReady | 208

Handling Type in ImageReady | 210

Rectangle and Ellipse Tools | 212

The ImageReady Optimise Palette | 213

Saving an Optimised Image | 215

Chapter Sixteen

Photoshop and ImageReady

ImageReady and Photoshop exist as separate application environments, but work side by side with one another. In some areas they overlap. Although both have area of distinct usage, they are deliberately similar in many respects, especially in the way in which much of the tool set, many of the palettes and working environment techniques are identical in both environments.

You can work on an image in Photoshop, then continue to make further adjustments to the same image in ImageReady, or vice versa. Use the Jump to button or command, covered on page 204, to move images seamlessly from one environment to the other so that you can work in the environment that gives you the most control for whatever task you are attempting.

The Animation, Slice and Rollover palettes are available in ImageReady only.

The majority of the ImageReady palettes have the same functionality as their conterparts in Photoshop.

The ImageReady Toolbox & Image Window

The ImageReady Toolbox is largely the same as the Photoshop Toolbox. This page indicates the tools found in ImageReady which are not found in Photoshop.

Slice tool, Slice Selection tool (see Chapter 18)

Rectangle Tool, Rounded Rectangle Tool, Ellipse Tool (see page 212)

Hide / Show Slices buttons (see Chapter 18)

Optimise Tabs

Status Bar Display pop-ups

View Percentage pop-up

Jumping Between Applications

Click the Hide Slices button to hide slice information and indicators.

See page 232 for information on hiding and showing slices.

You can start creating an image in either Photoshop or Image Ready, then use the Jump to command or button to move the image back and forth between working environments to suit your purposes as you work on the image, depending on the sorts of changes you want to make. Follow the guidelines below for moving images between applications.

1   For an image that you have started to prepare in Photoshop, either choose File > Jump to, then select Image Ready from the sub menu, or click the Jump to button.

Although you can work on an image in two different applications, there is only one image file. Changes you make in one environment can be used to update the image in the other environment. To avoid confusion - always ensure that changes you make in one environment are saved and that you update these changes to the image in the other environment when prompted.

2   If you have not saved the image in Photoshop, a prompt appears allowing you to do so. Click the Save button if you have previously saved and named the file. Click the Save as button if the file is not already saved. (See page 46 for information on saving files.

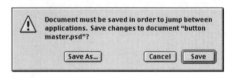

3   Image Ready then launches and the image appears in the ImageReady application window. You can now make further changes to the image in ImageReady. (The image remains open in the Photoshop application environment.)

4   To move the image currently active in ImageReady back into the Photoshop working environment, again, click the Jump

Individual or multiple changes you make in one application environment are represented in the History palette of the other application as a single entry called 'Update from File'.

to button, or choose File > Jump to, then select Adobe Photoshop from the sub menu.

5 You will be prompted to save any changes made to the file in ImageReady, before you are returned to Photoshop. Click the Save/Save as button as necessary.

Depending on which application environment is active, clicking on an image window of the other application also has the effect of the Jump to command.

6 A second prompt box appears, indicating the change made to the image outside of Photoshop. To avoid confusion, it is advisable to click the Update button so that the ImageReady version and the Photoshop version remain consistent.

Follow the same procedures outlined here when you create a new image in ImageReady and move it into Photohsop.

7 When you are moving an image between applications, both files in each application have the same file name. Think of this as having an active copy, the one you are working on in the currently active application environment, with the other file as a live backup. It is best, as far as possible, to keep these two files synchronised. The best way to achieve this is to choose File > Preferences > General. Select the Auto-Update files option.

Creating and Saving Images

Although creating and saving images in ImageReady is very similar to the same routines in Photoshop, there are some differences to be aware of.

In ImageReady New Document dialogue box there is no colour mode pop-up. Images in ImageReady are always in RGB mode.

1 To create a new file in ImageReady, choose File > New. Enter values in pixels for Width and Height, or change the existing values by clicking on the increment arrows. There is no need to give the file a name at this stage.

In the ImageReady New Document dialogue box you do not set a resolution. The resolution of images in ImageReady is always 72 ppi.

2 Choose an option for the Contents of First Layer. Select White to fill the default layer with White. Choose Background to fill the layer with the current Background colour. Choose Transparent to create a transparent layer.

3 To save a file, in the first instance, choose File > Save as. In the Save Original dialogue box, specify a location in which you want to save the file. Enter a name. Notice that the .psd file extension is automatically added to the file name. Make sure you retain the file extension. Click the Save button.

4 Continue to work on the file in

You work in Photoshop file format (.psd) as you build and edit an image. Optimise the image when you have finished working on it and want to prepare it for the WWW.

Photoshop format and use the Save command (Ctrl/Command+S) regularly to save changes you make.

5 Use the Status bar pop-ups to choose readouts that help you make decisions about the image on which you are working.

Make sure you are working in Original tab to edit and change the image.

6 When the image is finished and you want to save an optimised version for use on the World Wide Web or in a multimedia application, use the Save Optimised As command. (See page 215 for information on saving optimised files.)

Layer Effects in ImageReady

ImageReady's Layer Effects are largely similar to those in Photoshop, but there are some important differences to be aware of.

1 To create a layer effect, click on the layer you want to modify to select it.

2 In addition to options in the Layers > Layer Effects sub-menu, you can use the Layer Effects pop-up in the bottom of the Layers palette to choose an effect.

When you create a new image in ImageReady, the first, default layer is layer 1. ImageReady does not have a default Background layer as its first layer like Photoshop. When you move a Photoshop image into ImageReady, the Background layer is converted into Layer 0 and treated as any other layer.

3 Options for specifying aspects of the effect are located in the Effects palette which displays appropriate controls according to which effect is selected in the Layers palette pop-up. (See page 125 for information on Bevel and Emboss layer effects in Photoshop.)

4 Click the collapse triangle to hide the names of any layer effects applied to a layer. This is a useful space saving option in complex illustrations using multiple layer effects. Click the collapse/expand triangle to show any layer effects applied to the layer.

5 Drag a layer effect name into the Wastebasket in the Layers palette to delete it. Alternatively, select a layer effect name, then click the Wastebasket icon. Click Delete in the Warning prompt.

6 Click the eye icon to the left of the layer effect to turn the layer effect on or off.

7 The Bevel and Emboss and Gradient Pattern palettes have additional options which may not be showing. Choose Show Options from the pop-up menu, or click the expand button in the palette tab.

Handling Type in ImageReady

ImageReady does not have a Type Tool dialogue box for creating and editing type. In ImageReady, type is entered and edited directly on screen.

Choose the Vertical Type tool to create vertical type.

1 To enter type, choose the Type tool. Position your cursor in the image window, then click to place the text insertion point.

When you create type in ImageReady you do not access the Type Tool dialogue box as you do in Photohsop.

2 Enter type using the keyboard. The type automatically creates a new type layer in the Layers palette. The new layer is positioned above the previously active layer. Type appears formatted with the current settings in the Type palette.

3 To make changes to the formatting of type, select the Type tool, then drag across the text in the image window. You can highlight type in this way, even if the type layer is not active.

When choosing an anti-aliasing level for type, make sure you are viewing the image at actual size to get the best feel for how the type will appear when viewed by the end user.

4 To change type settings, choose Window > Show Type if the Type palette is not already showing. Enter settings to format type.

5 When a type layer is active, when you choose any tool other than the type tool, the type highlights with a blue line running across the base of the type and a small square indicating the current alignment setting for the type.

6 To reposition type, make sure the type layer is active, select the Move tool, then drag the type.

7 Choose Show options from the Type palette pop-up to access Baseline Shift and Rotation controls. Rotation is only available for Vertical type.

Rectangle and Ellipse Tools

Use the Rectangle, Rounded Rectangle and Ellipse tools to draw basic shapes. The techniques for using each tool are the same.

I To draw a rectangle or oval, choose the appropriate tool. Position your cursor in the image window, then press and drag to create the shape. Release the mouse when the object is the required size. The shape is placed on a new layer by default. The object fills with the current foreground colour.

Shapes you create with the shape tools are bitmap objects; not vector objects that you would create using similar tools in, for example, Adobe Illustrator.

2 To create a square or a circle, hold down Shift and drag with the shape tool. Start to drag with a shape tool, then hold down Alt, to draw a shape from the centre out.

3 Choose Window > Show Options to see the Options palette for the selected tool. Alternatively, double-click the tool to display the options palette.

4 Select Fixed Size to create a shape to precise dimensions.

5 Switch off the New Layer option if you do not want the tool to create a new layer for the shape automatically.

6 Choose anti-aliased (Ellipse and Rounded Rectangle) to help the object blend into its background by creating a slightly soft edge.

The ImageReady Optimise Palette

The basic principles for optimising images in ImageReady are the same as in Photoshop Save for Web dialogue box (see pages 186–189). The main difference is that the Original, Optimised, 2-Up and 4-Up tabs are part of the ImageReady window and therefore always available. The optimisation settings and controls are located in the Optimise palette.

The purpose of optimising an image is to create an acceptable balance between image quality and download times.

1 Choose Window > Show Optimise if the Optimise palette is not already showing.

2 Use the 2-Up and 4-Up tabs to compare the visual quality of different optimisation settings, along with file format, file size and downlaod time readouts. To hide or show annotations in the 2-Up/ 4-Up views, choose View > Hide/ Show Optimisation Info.

3 In 4-Up view, select an optimised version of the image – a black highlight border appears around the selected pane.

Choose Repopulate views from the pop-up menu in the Optimise palette. The selected version now becomes the Optimised version and ImageReady automatically generates two smaller, lower quality version of the optimised image in the two remaining panes.

4 When you begin working with Optmisation settings, use the predefined settings in the Settings pop-up as the basis for optimising images.

5 To restore an optimised version of the image to the original version, first select the optimised version, then choose Original from the Settings pop-up in the Optimise palette.

Saving an Optimised Image

When you have decided on optimisation settings that give you the correct balance between image quality and file size, you can then save an optimised version of the file.

1 Choose File > Save to save any changes to image in the original Photoshop file format.

2 If you are working with the Optimised tab selected, check that the current optimisation settings in the Optimise palette are the ones you want. Alternatively, choose Optimisation information from the Status bar pop-ups. Then choose File > Save Optimised As.

3 If you are working in 2-Up view, make sure the Optimised pane is selected. A selected pane is indicated by a black highlight border. Choose File > Save Optimised As.

4 If you are working with the 4-Up tab, make sure you select the pane with the settings you want to use for optimising the image. Then choose File > Save Optimised As.

If you are working on an optimised image, in 2-Up or 4-Up view, when you choose File > Save Optimised, the settings you save are those of the selected image pane.

5 In the Save Optimised dialogue box, specify a location and a name for the file. The appropriate file format extension (e.g. .gif) is appended automatically. Make sure you retain the file extension. Leave the Save Images option selected.

6 Select the Save HTML File option to save an additional HTML file that includes the image name, its dimensions in pixels and any other code necessary to display the image on a Web page. The HTML file is saved as a separate file with a .html extension in the same folder as the image file. This option is most useful when you are saving images with slices (see Chapter 18.)

7 Select the Save Selected Slices only when you have selected specific slices in the image prior to choosing the Save Optimised As command. ImageReady creates a complete HTML table capable of displaying the selected slices.

Animations

Animations are built from a series of GIF images which, when displayed in quick succession, create the illusion of movement. You create and control animations using the Animation and Layers palettes in ImageReady.

Animations can bring impact, movement and variety to a Web page, but they can also become distracting if not used carefully. Use animations when they bring dynamism to a page and contribute to the message and content. Don't use animations for their own sake.

Covers

Creating a Simple Animation | 218

Playing and Managing Frames | 220

Optimising and saving Animations | 222

Tweening | 224

Copying and Pasting Frames | 226

Chapter Seventeen

Creating a Simple Animation

Animations can range from the very simple to the very complex. Try to keep your animations simple at the outset. Remember that animation effects, if used indiscriminately on Web pages, can be distracting and as a result lose their intended impact.

When you open or create an image in ImageReady, the image becomes the first frame in the Animation palette by default, even if you do not intend to create an animation.

1　Create an image in Photoshop, or directly in ImageReady as in this example. Use Layers as the basis for the animation. The layers you create form the basic building blocks for the animation. Put elements you want to animate on separate layers.

To avoid confusion as you create an animation, make sure that you have created and finished editing all the objects and layers you want to use, before you start to build the animation.

2　Hide any layers containing elements you do not want to appear at the start of the animation.

3　Choose Window > Show Animation to show the Animation palette if it is not already showing. Choose New Frame from the palette's pop-up menu, or click the New Frame button. This creates frame 2, which is a duplicate of the preceding frame.

Animations are saved in GIF file format. JPEG and PNG formats cannot be used for animations.

4 Make a change to a layer. Changes you make to the layers, such as layer visibility, position, opacity or layer effects, form the animation when the frames are viewed in quick succession. In this example the 'P' is moved next to the 'U'.

When working in ImageReady, it is best to create and edit the animation in Original view. Options for editing animations are more limited in Optimised view.

5 Repeat Steps 3–4 as necessary. In this example, both the 'P' and 'U' are moved to the 'S'. Then, for the final frame, the 'P', 'U' and 'S' are moved up to the 'H'.

6 Save the animation in Photoshop format as you build and make changes. This means you can return to the original file, if necesary to make further adjustments. (See pages 222–223 for information on saving an optimised version of the animation for use on the Web.)

Any changes you make on a layer that affect actual pixel values, for example, painting, changing colour or tone, or using transform commands, will affect all frames in the animation in which the layer is present.

Playing and Managing Frames

As you build an animation you will need to preview it and to control aspects such as looping and frame rate.

To select multiple, consecutive frames, click on the first frame, hold down Shift, then click on the last frame in the range you want to select. To select nonconsecutive frames, click on a frame to select it, hold down Ctrl/Command, then click on other frames to add them to the previously selected frame.

1 To play an animation, click the Play button. The animation plays in the image window and each frame in the Animation palette highlights in sequence as the animation plays.

2 Click the Stop button to stop the animation at the current frame.

3 To select a frame, click on the frame in the Animation palette. The frame highlights and becomes the current frame. The current frame is displayed in the image window. It is the frame that can currently be edited.

When you select multiple frames, you can distinguish the current frame by the black highlight border around the frame.

4 To delete a frame, first click on it to select it. Then click the Wastebasket button at the bottom of the palette. Click the Delete button in the warning dialogue / prompt. Alternatively, drag the frame into the Wastebasket, or choose Delete Frame from the pop-up menu in the palette.

5 To change the position of a frame, select the frame you want to move, then drag it to a new location. Release the mouse when you see a thick black bar at the position to which you want to move the frame.

Preview animations in a browser to get an accurate idea of the delay you specify.

6 To set the frame delay rate (the speed at which frames advance), first select a frame, or multiple frames. Use the Frame Delay pop-up located below each frame. Either choose a value from the preset list, or choose other, then specify a delay in the Set Frame Delay dialogue box.

7 To specify looping options, use the Loop pop-up in the bottom left corner of the Animation palette. Forever plays the animation in a continuous loop. Choose Other to specify a set number of times you want the animation to play. Enter a value in the Play ... times field.

Optimising and Saving Animations

When you have created the frames for your animation and you are satisfied with the effect, you can optimise and then save the animation.

1 To optimise an animation, click the Optimise tab in the ImageReady window. In the Optimise palette, choose the optimisation settings you want to use from the Settings pop-up.

2 To preview the results of the optimisation settings, choose File > Preview in, then choose from the list of available browsers. The browser launches and the animation plays in the browser window.

File format information and HTML code are displayed below the animation for information purposes. Close the browser.

3 Test other optimisation settings and preview until you are satisfied with the results.

4 To save the animation, choose File > Save Optimised As. Use standard Macintosh/ Windows techniques to specify a location and a name for the file. Make sure you retain the .GIF file extension which should appear automatically.

5 Select the Save HTML file option if you want to save the HTML code for the animation file. The HTML file is saved in the same folder and with the same name as the animation, but with an HTML file extension.

6 Make sure you leave the Save Images option selected. Click the Save button.

Tweening

In ImageReady, the Tween command allows you to create smoother animations quickly and easily, by automatically creating additional frames between existing frames in the animation. These additional, in-between frames create smoother movement in the animation.

The term 'tweening' is derived from a traditional animation term 'in betweening' where additional frames were created between key frames to create smooth animation effects.

1. To tween a frame, first select the frame you want to tween. Choose Tween... from the pop-up menu in the Animation palette.

Use tweening to dramatically reduce the amount of time needed to create smooth animations.

2. For Layers, select the Selected Layers option to vary only the currently selected layer in the selected frame, otherwise leave the option set to All Layers.

3. Choose Parameter options to specify which elements you want to tween. In this example it is important to choose Position, as it is the position of the layers in the animation that vary. Select Opacity if opacity settings vary between frames. Select Effects if Layer Effects vary between frames.

4. Use the Tween with pop-up to choose the frame with which you want to tween the currently selected frame.

You can tween the last and first frames in an animation. This is useful to create a smooth transition from the end of an animation back to the beginning, when the animation is designed to loop a number of times.

5 Enter a value in the Frames to Add field to specify the number of in-between frames. The more in-between frames you add, the smoother the animation, but results in a larger file size.

6 OK the dialogue box. The in-between frames are added as new frames. Subsequent frames are renumbered accordingly.

Copying and Pasting Frames

You can copy a frame or multiple frames and then paste the copied frame(s) into a new location in the current animation, or into a completely different animation.

1 To copy a frame, first select the frame. A black highlight indicates the frame is selected.

2 Choose Copy Frame from the Animation palette pop-up menu.

3 Select a frame in which you want to paste the copied frame. Choose Paste Frame from the Animation pop-up menu.

4 Hold down Shift, then choose Paste Frame to paste the copied frame after the currently selected destination frame.

Slicing Images

Slicing allows you to create a single, complete image in Photoshop or ImageReady, then sub-divide it into specific areas – the slices. ImageReady automatically generates the HTML code for a table that will hold the sliced image.

Using slices you can optomise parts of an image differenlty for different purposes; slices can become buttons and assigned links; and you can also create rollover states for slices.

Covers

Slices from Guides and the Slice Tool | 228

Creating Slices from Selections | 230

User- and Auto-slices | 231

Working with Slices | 232

Assigning URLs to Slices | 234

Chapter Eighteen

Slices from Guides and the Slice Tool

Create the image in Photoshop if you need to work to a visible grid. Image Ready does not support grids.

Slices are rectangular areas of an image that become the contents of a single cell in an HTML table. An image in ImageReady initially consists of a single slice by default: comprising the complete image. When you create a new slice, the remainder of the image is automatically divided into further slices that will fit into an HTML table.

You can create slices based on ruler guides or selections, or you can create a slice using the Slice tool. This section looks at techniques for creating slices from guides and using the Slice tool.

When you use the Create Slices from Guides command, ImageReady deletes previously created slices.

Slices from Guides

1 Create or open an image. Drag in ruler guides to indicate where you want to create slices. (See page 27 for information on creating ruler guides.) Click the Jump to button if you are not already working in ImageReady.

Any image in ImageReady initially consists of one slice which is comprised of the entire image. When you create a new slice, ImageReady automatically divides the rest of the image into further, additional slices that will fit into a HTML table.

2 Choose Slices > Create Slices from Guides. The slices appear in the image. Each slice is numbered. Slices created from guides are User-slices. (See page 231 for information on User- and Auto-slices.) A colour adjustment, visible when slices are showing is applied to slices to indicate User- and Auto-slices. (See page 231 for further information.)

Slices you create using the Create Slices from Guides command and using the Slice tool are created as User-slices.

Slices are rectangular areas of an image that become the contents of individual cells in an HTML table. When loaded in a browser, the image appears to be a single, composite image. In HTML terms, it is split into discreet, separate areas.

3 Choose the Slice Selection tool (A), then click on a slice to select it. A coloured bounding box appears around the slice, defining the area of the slice.

4 The selected slice also appears in the Slice palette. Choose Window > Show Slice if the palette is not already showing.

The Slice Tool

1 To create a slice using the Slice tool, click on the tool to select it. Position your cursor on the image, then drag to define the area of the slice.

2 When you release the mouse, ImageReady automatically generates additional slices to enable the image to fit into an HTML table.

3 Hold down Shift as you drag with the Slice tool to create a square slice. Hold down Alt as you drag to create the slice from the centre out.

4 Choose Slice > Snap to Slices if you want the slice tool to snap to other slices or guides. The snap takes effect when your cursor comes within 4 pixels of a slice or guide.

Creating Slices from Selections

You can also create slices from selections.

1 Create a selection. Choose Slice > Create Slice from Selection. The selection becomes a User-slice. (See page 231 for information on User and Auto-slices.) The User-

page 231 for

When you click the Hide Slices button (Q), the colour adjustments applied to slices disappears.

slice is numbered and the remainder of the image is divided into further slices as necessary to fit the complete image into an HTML table. The user-slice is selected and a highlight bounding box appears around it. A colour adjustment is applied to the remainder of the image. This colour adjustment is helpful in distinguishing between user- and auto-slices.

2 Continue creating slices as necessary.

User- and Auto-slices

A slice can have one of two statuses: User or Auto. There are more possibilities for modifying User-slices. Any slices you create (using guides, selections or the Slice tool) are User-slices. Slices created automatically by ImageReady to enable the remainder of the image to fit into an HTML table are Auto-slices. An image in ImageReady automatically consists of one auto-slice compromising the full image.

You can change or 'promote' an auto-slice into a user-slice. User-slices can be assigned different optimisation settings. Auto-slices in an image are initially linked and therefore share the same optimisation settings. The link symbol which appears next to auto-slices indicates that they share the same optimisation settings.

There are two types of slices: Image or No Image. Image slices contain image information – pixels. No Image slices can contain a solid colour, or HTML text. An Image slice is identified by the image icon when slices are visible.

Starting in the top left corner, slices are numbered from left to right and top to bottom. As you add, delete and rearrange slices, slice numbers are updated automatically.

The colour adjustment applied to slices dims the brightness and contrast of unselected slices. This is for display purposes only. The colour adjustment does not affect the final colour of images.

Different colour adjustments on User- and Auto-slices and the slice information icons help you distinguish the two statuses. The colour adjustment on User-slices is half the strength of the colour adjustment used to distinguish Auto-slices.

Working with Slices

Use the following techniques to hide and show slices and to select and deselect slices.

Slices show automatically when you select the Slice Select tool.

1 To hide slices and slice information such as slice number and slice type icons, click the Hide Slice button (Q) in the Toolbox. To show slices, click the Show Slice button (Q).

2 To select a slice, select the Slice Select tool (A). Click on a slice. A coloured bounding box with eight selection handles appears around the slice indicating it is selected. The colour adjustment, which defines the area of the slices, is switched off for the selected slice.

When you add, delete or rearrange slices, ImageReady recomposes the HTML table accordingly.

3 To select multiple slices, select a slice, hold down Shift, then click inside another slice to add it to the selection.

4 When you select a slice, it appears in the Slice palette. Choose Window > Show Slice to show the Slice palette if it is not already showing. The slice number and file format of the slice are indicated below the slice thumbnail. (See page 234 for information on assigning URLs to slices so that they can function as buttons on a Web page.)

When you show slices, a colour adjustment is applied to the slices to indicate areas that constitute a slice.

5 Choose File >
Preview in, then
select a Browser
from the sub-
menu to preview
the image in the
browser window.
The automatically
generated HTML
code for the table
that contains the
slices is also
displayed in the browser window.

6 Use the Optimise palette to create optimisation settings for
the image. (See Chapter 16 for details). You can create
different optimisation settings for individual slices if required.

7 Choose Save Optimised As to save an optimised version of
the image. (See page 216 for information on saving
optimised images).

Assigning URLs to Slices

You make a slice act as a clickable button that will link to another Web page by assigning a URL to the slice.

1 Select the Slice tool. Click on a slice to select it. Make sure the Slice palette is showing (Window > Show Slice). The selected slice appears in the palette.

When you assign a URL to an auto-slice it becomes a user-slice.

2 The slice is automatically named with the file name of the image,

followed by an underscore and its slice number.

3 Enter a URL in the URL entry field. You should include the http:// specifier at the beginning of the URL. You can choose any previously created URL from the URL pop-up menu.

4 If you are preparing images for a Web site that uses frames,

specify a target frame – where the HTML file you link to will appear – using the Target entry field. Enter the name of the target frame exactly as defined in the frameset file.

Index

Adaptive palette   193
Add Noise filter   181
Add Point tool   151
Additive primaries   11
Adjustment layers   121
Adobe Gamma utility   18
Adobe Gamma Wizard   18
Adobe Illustrator   154
Adobe PageMaker   13
Airbrush tool   77
Aligning elements   27
Alpha channels   160
　　Masks   162
Anchor points   148, 150, 153
Animations
　　Animation palette   218
　　Copy and paste frames   226
　　Current frame   220
　　Frame delay rate   221
　　Layers   218
　　Loop pop-up   221
　　New Frame button   218
　　Optimising   222
　　Play button   220
　　Stop button   220
　　Tween command   224
Anti-aliased   44, 81, 84, 94, 99, 102
Apple RGB. *See* RGB Setup
Arrowheads   79
Auto erase   78
Auto Levels   169
Auto-Update files   205

Background colour   64–66, 70
Background Eraser Tool   95
Behind   82
Bit-depth   9
Bitmaps   8
Black Ink. *See* Greyscale Setup
Blending mode   77–78, 81–82
Blur More filter   179

Blur tool   86
Border, adding   59
Brightness   168
　　Graph   172
Brightness and Contrast   19
Brush
　　Defining   84
　　Options   72
Burn tool   90

Channels   159–163, 166
　　Options   166
　　Palette   159, 162
Clipping paths   48, 152, 154
Clone   88
　　Non-aligned   89
Close box/icon   30
Clouds filter   164
CMYK Colour Model   11
CMYK Setup   15
Colour   63–70, 167–174
　　Balance   174
　　Bar   69
　　Burn   83
　　Cast   174
　　Correction   167–174
　　Dodge   83
　　Gamut   12
　　Models (CMYK and RGB)   11
　　Palette   69
　　Picker   66
Colour Management Module   16
Colour Sampler Tool   65
Composite channel   159
Concavity   79
Convert-anchor-point Tool   151
Create Layer command   128
Creating a new file   50
Crop marquee   58
Crop tool   58
Cursor location   29

Cursor types   75
Curves   172–173
   Segments   148
Custom palette   193

Darken   83
Default Colours icon   64
Defringe command   111
Despeckle filter   182
Difference   83
Direct Selection tool   150–151, 153
Direction point   148, 150–151, 153
Display Using Monitor Compensation   14
Dissolve   82
Dithering   195
Document sizes   26
Dodge tool   90
Drawing lines   79
Duotone   62
Dust & Scratches filter   182

Edge Contrast. *See* Magnetic Lasso Tool
Edge Highlighter Tool   131
Edges   177
Edit > Copy   110, 113
Edit > Define Pattern   89, 112
Edit > Fill   50, 112
Edit > Paste   113
Edit > Paste Into   110
Edit > Purge Histories   37
Edit > Undo   36
Ellipse Tool   212
Elliptical Marquee tool   98
Encoding   48
EPS files
   Opening   44
   Placing   45
Eraser tool   92
Exact palette   193
Export Paths dialogue box   156
Exposure   74, 90
Extract command   131
Eyedropper Options palette   65
Eyedropper tool   65, 75

Fade   74, 76
Fastening Points   103
Feather   99, 102, 106–107
File > Colour Settings > CMYK Setup   15
File > Colour Settings > Greyscale Setup   17
File > Colour Settings > RGB Setup   14
File > Image Info   34
File > Jump to   204
File > New   50
File > Open   40, 113
File > Page Setup   35
File > Place   45
File > Preferences > Display and Cursors   75
File > Preview in   222
File > Print   34
File > Revert   36
File > Save   36, 46
File > Save As   46
File > Save Optimised As   223
File > TWAIN Acquire   41
File > TWAIN Select Source   41
File formats   13, 47
   EPS   13, 48
   GIF   196–198
   JPEG   49, 199
   Photo CD   42
   PNG   200
   TIFF   13, 47
Fill dialogue box   112
Fill Tool   132
Filter controls   176
Finger painting   87
Flatness   154
Focoltone matching system   68
Focus Tools   86
Foreground colour   64–66, 70
Full screen mode   22
Full screen with menu bar mode   22

Gamma   14, 171
Gamut alarm   66, 69
Gaussian blur   179
Gradient tool   80
Greyscale Setup   17
Grow command   109

Halftone screen settings   10
Hand tool   28
Hard light   83
Hardness   72
Hide Slice button   232
History Palette
   Clearing States   37
   Deleting States   37
   History State   36
   Purging States   37
   Snapshots   36
   Taking Snapshots   38
Hue   83

ICC (International Colour Consortium)   15
Image > Canvas Size   59
Image > Extract   131
Image > Image Size   53–54, 56
Image > Rotate Canvas   52
Image > Rotate Canvas > Arbitrary   52
Image modes   60
   Bitmap   61
   CMYK   13, 60
   Duotone   61
   Greyscale   61
   Indexed Colour   60
   LAB   61
   RGB   13, 60
Image resolution   10
Image size
   Resizing (and resolution)   8–9
     Resampling   53–57
Image window   23
ImageReady   202
   Animations   217
   Optimise tab   222
   Optimised view   219
   Slicing   227
   Toolbox   203
Indexed Colour mode   192
Info palette   29
Input levels   170
Interlaced option   196, 198
International Colour Consortium   18
Interpolation   54

JPEG format   49, 199
Jump to button/command   22, 25, 202, 204

Lasso Tool   100, 102
Lasso Width. *See* Magnetic Lasso Tool
Layer > Effects > Clear Effects   128
Layer > Effects > Set Global Angle   127
Layer > Matting > Defringe   111
Layer > Merge Down   118
Layer > Merge Visible   118
Layer > New > Adjustment   121
Layer > New > Layer Via Cut   101
Layer > Type > Render Layer   137
Layer Effects   125, 208 (ImageReady)
   Applying   125
   Bevel and Emboss   125
   Editing   127
   Global Angle   127
   Managing   127
   Merging   127
Layers   116
   Deleting   116
   Flattening   118
   Hiding   117
   Linking   120
   Masks   110, 164
   Merging   118
   Moving between images   119
   New Layer command   116
   Options   116
   Palette   116
   Reordering   117
   Repositioning   117
   Selecting   117
   Showing   117
   Transform   129
   Transparency   123
   Unlinking   120
Layers > Layer Effects   208
Layers palette   210
Levels dialogue box   170
Lighten   83
Line width   79

Load Selection dialogue box   161
Loading settings   32
Luminosity   83
LZW compression   47

Magic Eraser Options/Tool   93
Magic Wand Tool   105
Magnetic Lasso Options   104
Magnetic Lasso Tool   103
Make Work Path icon   146
Marquee selection Tool   98–99
Mask icon   164
Median filter   182
Merge Down command   118
Merge Visible command   118
Monitor Calibration   18
Motion Blur   179
Move Tool   100, 124, 211
Multiply   82

Navigator palette   28
New Adjustment Layer command   121
New Channel icon   161
New Layer dialogue box   116
New Layer Via Copy command   124
New Layer Via Cut command   124
New Snapshot command   38

Opacity   74, 81, 83
Open As command   40
Options palettes   75
Output levels   171
Overlay   82

Paint Bucket Tool   81
Paintbrush Tool   76
Palettes   30
   Brushes   72, 84
   Choosing/resizing   30–31
Pantone matching system   68

Paths   145–156
   Closed   149
   Creating   148
   Deleting   150
   Deselecting   150
   Direction line   149
   Exporting   156
   Open   149
   Palette   146, 150, 154
   Selecting   150
   Showing   150
Pattern Stamp Tool   89
Patterns, aligned/non-aligned   89
Pen Tool   148
Pencil Tool   78
Photo CD   42
Photoshop EPS   155
Pixel   10
Points
   Adding   151
   Converting   151
   Corner points   151–152
   Editing   153
   Smooth point   151
Polygon Lasso Tool   102
PostScript   9
Precise cursors   25
Preserve Luminosity option   174
Preserve Transparency option   123
Pressure   74, 83
Preview   48
Printing
   ASCII Encoding   34
   Background   33
   Binary Encoding   34
   Bleed button   33
   Border button   33
   Calibration Bars   35
   Chooser   33
   Composite Image   33
   Composites (Windows)   35
   JPEG Encoding   35
   Orientation   33, 35
   Page Setup   33
   Paper Size   35
   PostScript Options   34

Printer resolution   10, 18
Screen button   33
Transfer button   33
Profile   15, 19
Progressive JPEG. *See* JPEG format
Proxy Preview   28

QuarkXPress   13, 154
Quick Mask mode   158
Quick Mask options   166

Raster   8
Rectangle Tool   212
Rectangular Marquee Tool   98
Resample Image option   53–57
Resampling   53
Resampling down   56
Resampling up   54
Reset button   176
Reshaping masks   163
Resizing images   53
Resolution   10
Reveal All   164
Revert/From Saved commands   26
RGB Colour Model   11
RGB Setup   14
Rotating   52
Rounded Rectangle Tool   212
Roundness   72
Rubber Band option   148
Rubber Stamp Tool   88
Ruler guides   27, 52
Rulers   23

Sample Merged option   81, 87
Sampling down   56
Saturation   83, 90
Save Optimised As command   207
Save Path command   147
Saving custom settings   32
Saving files   46

EPS   48
JPEG   49
Photoshop format   46
TIFF   47
Scanning into Photoshop   41
Scratch disk   26
Screen   82
Screen modes   22
Scroll bars   28
Secondary colours   11
Select > Deselect   100
Select > Feather   106
Select > Grow   109
Select > Hide Edges   108
Select > Inverse   107
Select > None   98
Select > Show Edges   108
Select > Similar   109
Selections   97–114
Adding to   108
Converting to paths   146
Copying   113
Deselecting   98
Distort   114
Filling   112
Inverse   113
Loading   160
Marquee   98
Modifying   108
Moving   100
Pasting   113
Pasting into   110
Repositioning   98
Rotate   114
Saving   160
Scale   114
Shear   114
Subtracting from   108
Transforming   114
Selection icon   161
Sharpen Edges   178
Sharpen filters   177
Sharpen Tool   86
Show Slice button   232
Similar command   109
Sizes bar   23, 26

Slice > Create Slice from Selection   230
Slice Selection Tool   229
Slice Tool   228, 234
Slices   228
  Assigning URLs   234
  Auto-slices   228, 230–231
  Image slice   231
  No Image slice   231
  Selecting   232
  Slice palette   229, 232
  User-slices   228, 230–231
Slices > Create Slices from Guides   228
Soft light   82
Source point   88
Spacing   72
Sponge Tool   91
Standard Mode icon   158
Swatches palette   70
Switch Colours icon   64
System palette   193

TIFF preview   155
Tolerance   81, 105, 109, 146
Tonal balance   170
Toning Tools   90
TWAIN interface   41
Type   135–144
  Alignment   136
  Anti-Aliased   138
  Baseline Shift   139
  Colour   136
  Converting Type Layers   137
  Editable Type Layer   137
  Editing   140
  Font   136, 138
  Kerning   139
  Leading   136, 138
  Preview   136
  Rotated   142
  Selecting   140
  Size   136, 138
  Style   136
  Tracking   139
Type Mask Tool   143
Type Tool   136, 210 (ImageReady)

Underlying pixels   100
Undo buffer. *See* History Palette
Unsharp Mask   52, 177
URL. *See* Slices
Use All Layers   89, 94

Vector applications   8
Vertical Type Tool   136, 142
Vignette, creating   107
Virtual memory   26
Visible grid   27
Visible spectrum   12

Web palette   193
Wet edges (Paintbrush & Eraser)   76
White Point   14
Window > Show Animation   218
Window > Show Layers   120
Window > Show Options   99
Window > Show Type   211
Work path   146, 148
World Wide Web   20, 192, 207

Zoom Tool   28